General editor: Graham Hand

CU00658867

Brodie's Notes on Chaucer's
The Pardoner's Tale

P. Gooden BA
English Department, Kingswood School, Bath

Pan Books London, Sydney and Auckland

This revised edition published 1986 by
Pan Books Ltd,
Cavaye Place, London SW10 9PG
9 8 7 6 5 4 3
© Pan Books Ltd 1986
ISBN 0 330 50237 9
Photoset by Parker Typesetting Service, Leicester
Printed and bound in Great Britain by
Richard Clay Ltd, Bungay, Suffolk

Contents

Preface

This student revision aid is based on the principle that any close examination of Chaucer's text is essential to a full understanding of his artistry. He is by common agreement one of our greatest comic poets, and *The Canterbury Tales* is his masterpiece. But because his language is not easy to understand, some due attention must be given to it and the ways in which it differs from our language today. Consequently each editor of a parallel text Chaucer in this series will give an account of Chaucer's grammar, versification and pronunciation.

The full text of the *Tale* will be given on the left hand side of the page, and opposite this there will be a colloquial prose translation. This must not be regarded as a 'crib'. Students should read it carefully against the original, consulting the glossary and textual notes in order to arrive at a full understanding of the meaning and, one hopes, of the nature of Chaucer's art. That art will be examined by each editor, who will deal with Chaucer's characterization, his humour, his narrative skills, the images he uses, indeed any aspect of his work which merits critical attention and comment. And further, when one has learned to read Chaucer and appreciate him, some knowledge will be necessary of the age in which he lived, and his place in it if that appreciation is to be extended. There will be a brief account of Chaucer's life and times, and the student is advised to look carefully at the textual notes and the critical commentary mentioned above. Revision questions and general questions are also included, and there will be a guideline note-form answer to one of the questions. The aim is not merely to prepare the student thoroughly for an examination, but also to introduce him to the challenge and delight of Chaucer by involving him directly with the text. That text is its own reward, for both the *Prologue* and the *Tales* are among the greatest imaginative literature of all time.

Graham Handley

Literary terms used in these notes

Irony

Irony is easier to detect in practice than it is to define. One (broad) definition would be that irony is the exploitation of the gap between the way things appear and the way they really are. If we had read only *The Pardoner's Tale* we might accept the poem as, among other things, a vigorous and sincerely felt denunciation of various sins. With the knowledge given us by *The Prologue* of the Pardoner's real nature, we are aware of an ironic contradiction between the tale and its teller. Much irony is unperceived by the person who is its 'victim'; for example, a figure in a novel or play might compliment himself or criticize others while we, as readers or audience, will be conscious that the compliment is inappropriate (a coward might claim to be a brave man, like Falstaff in *Henry IV*) or that the criticism of others would be better directed at the speaker himself. Irony can be complex. In *The Pardoner's Tale* the three revellers form a brotherhood and swear to 'live and die for each other', an ironic pledge in two ways, firstly because the idea of a brotherhood vanishes when they find the gold and start to plot against each other, and secondly because the trio do indeed 'die for each other' not in a spirit of self-sacrifice but out of greed.

A brief description of Chaucer's life and works

Geoffrey Chaucer was born about 1340 near the Tower of London. He was born into the age of Edward III, and of the Black Prince, into the Age of Chivalry and the magnificent court of Edward III with knights and ladies, heraldry and tournaments, minstrels and poetry, music and story-telling.

Chaucer entered into this rich and colourful courtly world at an early age, when he became a page in the household of the Countess of Ulster, wife to Lionel, later Duke of Clarence, and one of the sons of Edward III. This was clearly arranged by his parents, who had some contacts at Court. His mother's first husband had been Keeper of the King's Wardrobe, and there can be little doubt that she had something to do with the appointment of Chaucer's father as deputy to the King's Butler. The first record of Geoffrey Chaucer appears in an account book, dating from 1357, which records a payment by the royal household to a London tailor for a cloak, multi-coloured breeches and a pair of shoes for the young page Chaucer. It was in the Duke's great houses in London and Yorkshire that the young page would have learned the elegant and aristocratic code of manners, and made the acquaintance of the high and the noble. He would have learned French and Latin, the languages of the Court, the Church and the educated classes. It was also one of the duties of a page to play and sing, and to recite poetry.

The next record we have is that Chaucer was taken prisoner by the French in 1359, during one of the campaigns in The Hundred Years' War, and ransomed in the following year – the King himself contributing £16 (a very large sum in those days) of the money. So Chaucer must have seen active service in the French wars, probably as a squire attending on one of the nobles, like the squire in the *Canterbury Tales* who attended on the Knight, his father. For the upper classes, the experience of being a prisoner of war in the Age of Chivalry was not too uncomfortable. It was normal for the 'prisoner' to be entertained as a 'house guest' until the ransom was paid, and it is probable that during this enforced stay in France Chaucer became thoroughly versed in French literature, particularly the *Roman de la rose* (the procedure manual, as it were, for 'courtly love'), which was to have such an important influence on his literary work.

After his ransom was paid, Chaucer returned to his Court duties, and was soon in a more elevated position. He became one of the valets in attendance on the King. In 1366 his father died and his mother married again. It is probable that in the same year he married Philippa, daughter of Sir Payne Roet and sister of Katherine Swynford, the mistress and later third wife to John of Gaunt. Philippa was a lady-in-waiting to the Queen. As a valet to the King, Chaucer would carry candles 'before the King', tidy up his bedroom and attend to a variety of duties which were to become more and more concerned with affairs of state. In 1386 he was sent abroad on the official business of the Crown. About this time he was promoted from valet to palace official. It appears that Chaucer went soldiering again in 1369, probably on one of John of Gaunt's campaigns in Picardy. In 1370 he was abroad again on the King's service, and we can now see him becoming a trusted civil servant as he was frequently sent on missions to France, Flanders and Italy. During his visits to Italy on official business Chaucer took the opportunity to become familiar with Italian literature, most especially the works of Petrarch, Boccaccio and Dante, which were to influence much of his subsequent poetry.

In 1374 he was promoted to a senior position as Comptroller of Customs and Subsidy (for wool, skins and hides) at the Port of London, and the City of London bestowed on him the lease of a house in Aldgate.

From about 1380 Chaucer settled down to his life as senior customs official, as there is only one record of further journeys abroad. He must have been respected as a man of affairs, as he became a Justice of the Peace in 1385, and a Member of Parliament, or Knight of the Shire for Kent, soon afterwards.

It was during these years that Chaucer found time to write seriously. His early literary attempts were influenced considerably by French literature. Then, when John of Gaunt left the country in 1386 on an adventure to claim the crown of Castile, the King's uncle, the Duke of Gloucester, took charge of the country's affairs (Richard being not yet of age), and Chaucer suffered from the new influences in royal patronage. He lost his

Comptrollership of Customs, he was not re-elected to Parliament and he had to give up his house in Aldgate. We even learn that he felt himself in danger of being sued for debt. Chaucer had now plenty of time to ponder and at this time he must have been preparing *The Canterbury Tales*.

In 1389 a rumour was abroad that the great Duke of Lancaster (Chaucer's patron John of Gaunt) was returning home. This helped the young King Richard II in taking over the reins of power from his uncle Gloucester. It has been stated that the young King Richard knew Chaucer and liked his poetry. There must be some substance in this, as shortly afterwards Chaucer was appointed Clerk of the King's Works. John of Gaunt returned to England in November 1389, and for the rest of his life Chaucer was to enjoy royal patronage and a comfortable living. It was in these years of semi-retirement that *The Canterbury Tales* were written. Alas, Chaucer died without having finished his masterpiece. His tomb in Westminster Abbey gives the date of his death – October 1400.

It seems probable that 1387 was the approximate date of commencement for *The Canterbury Tales*. Chaucer's renown rests mainly on this work, but in terms of volume the *Tales* form less than half of his writing which has come down to us. Besides a number of shorter poems, there are five other major works in verse and two or three in prose. Chaucer's most important production during his first tentative years as a writer was the translation he probably made of the *Roman de la Rose*, the style and content of which was to have such a great influence on his writing. His first major poem was *The Book of the Duchess*, a poem steeped in the French tradition, written about 1370 to commemorate the death of Blanche, Duchess of Lancaster, and wife of his patron, John of Gaunt. This was the first of four love-vision poems, the others being *The House of Fame*, *The Parliament of Fowls* and *The Legend of Good Women* (whose date is doubtful). Chaucer's works can be conveniently grouped into three parts, the French period, the Italian period and the English period; and, generally speaking, the periods follow one another in chronological sequence. The French period showed the influence of the *Roman de la Rose*, and included the love-vision poems. The Italian period (1380–5), is marked by the narrative poem *Troilus and Criseyde*, which rehandles a theme of the Italian poet Boccaccio. *Troilus and Criseyde* is a masterpiece, and is still considered to be the finest narrative poem in English, full of beauty and lyrical quality, and delightful humour in the character of Pandarus. The English period (1389–1400) is the last, and is the period when Chaucer reached his full maturity as a dramatic poet. This is the period of *The Canterbury Tales*, a collection of tales and tellers that is unique in English literature. Chaucer died before he could complete this great masterpiece.

It must be emphasized that these terms, 'French,' 'Italian', 'English' for Chaucer's literary life only indicate predominant influences: the stories in *The Canterbury Tales* are drawn from far and wide; *The Knight's Tale*, for instance, again owes its theme to a story by Boccaccio.

Setting and plot of the *Tale*

Setting

In his Prologue to *The Canterbury Tales* Chaucer tells us that he had already taken up his quarters at the Tabard Inn, Southwark, preparatory to beginning the next day his pilgrimage to Canterbury Cathedral, when twenty-nine others appeared at the Inn, intent on the same purpose. These had presumably met one another as they converged upon London, and soon adopted the poet as a member of their party. The host, Harry Bailly, realizing that this company was the pleasantest he had seen in the tavern that year, proposed that they should while away the tedium of the journey of two days by telling one another stories, suggesting that each should tell two on the outward and two on the homeward way. The proposal was adopted without a dissentient, and as the Host announces his intention of travelling with his guests, they appointed him judge of the tales and general referee. They approved his plan that the teller of the best tale should be entertained at supper, at the Tabard, at the expense of the others, on their return. The company then retired to bed and commenced the journey the next morning early. A mile or so along the Kent Road the Host pulled up by a brook, where it was decided by lot that the Knight, the most distinguished of the party, should tell the first tale. Eleven tales had been told before the Host called upon the Physician to entertain the company. His story of Appius and Virginia depressed them, the Host asserting that his heart was lost 'for pitee of this mayde'. He appealed therefore to the Pardoner to tell something amusing as a restorative. The better people on the pilgrimage, having by now some knowledge of the Pardoner's disreputable character, protested at the invitation, but it was accepted. After partaking of refreshment at a wayside alestake, the Pardoner gave a sample of his pulpit oratory, and included the excellent story of 'The Three Revellers', which some critics have called the best short story in the world.

Scholars have divided the tales told on the way to Canterbury into nine groups, and have placed this tale in group three, where it follows that told by the Doctor. The text in this edition follows the numbering usually recognized and begins with line 287. The previous 286 lines contain the Physician's tale; lines 287 to 328 record the conversation between the Host and the Pardoner which follows the Host's expression of disgust at the treatment of Virginia in the story he had just heard. The *Prologue to the Pardoner's Tale* occupies lines 329 to 462, after which the Pardoner introduces his narrative. He digresses after a very few lines into a denunciation of the sins of gluttony, gambling, and swearing, but returns to his story with line 661 and brings it to a close with line 894. The remaining lines show the man at his professional practice, trying by various means to rake in money from his fellow pilgrims, who have been enjoying his illustration of the dire results of the excessive love of wealth.

Plot

The story – as distinct from the *Prologue* – which Chaucer provides for the Pardoner is not original, although some of its detail is the author's invention. The narrative is startlingly bare. Three young 'revellers', who spend their lives in drinking, gambling etc., hear of the sudden death of an acquaintance. Acting as if Death were a real person, they go searching in order to put an end to 'him'. In their drunken rage they encounter, not Death, but an old man who points them to the place where they will discover the object of their quest. Following the old man's direction they find a hoard of gold under an oak tree. They forget their search for Death, and the youngest of the three goes off to fetch some provisions while the other two watch over the treasure; in his absence they plot to kill him to get the larger share for themselves. Meanwhile the youngest has hit upon the idea, in his turn, of disposing of his two partners. He returns with bottles of poisoned wine; they stab him according to plan; then they decide to relax before burying their companion's body, and drink from the poisoned bottles. They die rapidly and in agony. Death has found all three.

The Pardoner's Tale in Chaucer's Middle English with a translation into modern English

The Character of The Pardoner

With him ther was a gentil PARDONER
Of Rouncival, his freend and his compeer,   670
That streight was comen fro the court of Rome.
Ful loude he song, *Com hider, love, to me.*
This somnour bar to him a stif burdoun,
Was never trompe of half so greet a soun.

This Pardoner hadde heer as yelow as wex,   675
But smothe it heng, as dooth a strike of flex;
By ounces henge his lokkes that he hadde,
And therwith he his shuldres overspradde;
But thinne it lay, by colpons, oon and oon;
But hood, for jolitee, he wered noon,   680
For it was trussed up in his walet.
Him thoughte he rood al of the newe jet;
Dischevele, save his cappe, he rood al bare.
Swiche glarynge eyen hadde he as an hare.
A vernicle hadde he sowed upon his cappe;   685
His walet lay biforn him in his lappe
Bret-ful of pardon, come from Rome al hoot.
A voys he hadde as smal as hath a goot;
No berd hadde he, ne never sholde have,
As smothe it was as it were late y-shave;   690
I trowe he were a geldyng or a mare.

The character of the Pardoner

Alongside him rode his close friend, a noble Pardoner from Ronces-valles, who had come straight from the court of Rome and who sang, 'Come hither, my love, to me' at the top of his voice, the Summoner accompanying him with such a strong droning bass that a trumpet could never make half as much noise

The Pardoner's wax-coloured hair hung smoothly like a hank of flax and fell in bunches of thin locks which spread over his shoulders. He wore no hood but carried it in his bag for it seemed more festive and fashionable to him to ride bare-headed, save for a cap, on which he had sewn a copy of St Veronica's handkerchief. His eyes glared like a hare's and his voice was as small as a goat's. As he had just lately come back from Rome, he had a bag, brimful of pardons, all hot and ready for sale, hanging in front of him on his lap. He had no beard nor was he likely to have one, as his chin was as smooth as if it had only just been shaved. Indeed, I believe he was a gelded horse or a mare.

But of his craft, fro Berwyk unto Ware,
Ne was ther swich another pardoner,
For in his male he hadde a pilwe-beer,
Which that, he seyde, was Oure Lady veyl;   695
He seyde he hadde a gobet of the seyl
That Seint Peter hadde whan that he wente
Upon the see til Jhesu Crist him hente.
He hadde a croys of latoun ful of stones,
And in a glas he hadde pigges bones.   700
But with thise relikes, whan that he fond
A poure person dwellynge up on lond,
Upon a day he gat him more moneye
Than that the person gat in monthes tweye;
And thus with feyned flaterye and japes   705
He made the person and the peple his apes.
But, trewely to tellen atte laste,
He was in chirche a noble ecclesiaste;
Wel coude he rede a lessoun or a storie,
But alderbest he song an offertorie,   710
For well he wiste, whan that song was songe,
He moste preche and wel affyle his tonge
To wynne silver, as he full well coude;
Therefore he song so merily and loude.

But there was no other pardoner from Berwick to Ware like him in the profession, for he carried in his bag a pillow-case, which, so he claimed, was Our Lady's veil. He declared that he had a piece of the sail belonging to the ship which St Peter had at the time he walked on the Sea of Galilee till Jesus Christ saved him, a cross of latten, ornamented with semi-precious stones, and the bones of a pig in a glass. When he came upon a poor *parson* living in a remote district, he gained for himself with these relics more money than the parson earned in two months and so, by means of false flattery and tricks, he made fools of the parson and his flock.

To sum up, he was not only a capable preacher in Church but also had ability in reading a passage from the Scriptures or a legend of a Saint. Best of all he sang an offertory for he knew that, after the anthem was sung, he had to preach and use a glib tongue to gain money. He could do this excellently and so he sang cheerfully and loudly.

The Wordes Of The Host
To The Phisicien And The Pardoner

Oure Hoostë gan to swere as he were wood: 287
'Harrow!' quod he, 'by naylës, and by blood,
This was a fals cherl and a fals justise!
As shameful deeth as hertë may devyse   290
Come to thise jugës, and hire advocatz!
Algate this sely mayde is slayn, allas!
Allas, to deerë boughtë she beautee!
Wherfore I seye al day, as men may see,
That yiftës of Fortune and of Nature   295
Been cause of deeth to many a creäture.
[Hire beautee was hire deth, I dar wel sayn;
Allas! so pitously as she was slayn!]
Of bothë yiftës that I speke of now
Men han ful oftë moorë harm than prow.   300

'But trewëly, myn owenë maister deere,
This is a pitous talë for to heere;
But nathëlees, passe over, is no fors;
I pray to God so save thy gentil cors,
And eek thyne urinals and thy jurdones   305
Thyn ypocras, and eek thy galiones,
And every boyste ful of thy letuarie;
God blesse hem, and oure lady Seint Marie!
So moot I theen, thou art a proprë man,
And lyk a prelat, by Seint Ronyan!   310
Seyde I nat wel? I kan nat speke in terme,
But wel I woot thou doost myn herte to erme,
That I almoost have caught a cardynacle.
By corpus bonës, but I have triacle,
Or elles a draughte of moyste and corny ale,   315
Or but I heere anon a myrie tale,
Myn herte is lost for pitee of this mayde.

The words of the Host
to the Physician and the Pardoner

Our Host began to swear as if he were mad. 'By heavens!' he exclaimed, 'by the nails and blood of Christ, I think he was a false fellow, and, what is more, it was a false judgment as well! My only hope is that the most shameful death ingenuity can devise will befall such judges and their counsels. Though, at any rate, that innocent maiden has unfortunately met her death, I consider she paid too dearly for her beauty. Therefore, I am always maintaining that the gifts of Fortune or of Nature have caused many a person's death, as people can see for themselves. I maintain that she died because she was so beautiful. Alas! she came to a pitiful death but from both the gifts I have just mentioned people very often derive more harm than good.

But, still, my own dear master, that was a sad story to which we have just listened. Even so, let us say no more about it as it does not really matter. I pray to God that he will protect your own noble body, and also your containers for urine and your chamber-pots, your Hippocrateses and your Galens and every box full of your ointment. I hope that God and our lady Saint Mary will bless them. By my desire to flourish, you are a fine-looking man and, by St Ninian, you remind me of an ecclesiast! Have I put my foot in it? I am pretty poor at technical terms but I know only too well that you have caused me such heartache that I have almost got palpitations! By the body and bones of Our Lord, I swear that, unless I have some remedy for it or at least have a draught of new beer that really tastes of barley-corn or unless I hear some cheerful story straightaway, my heart will be overwhelmed out of sheer pity for this girl.

Thou beel amy, thou Pardoner,' he sayde.
'Tell us som myrthe or japës right anon!'
　'It shal be doon,' quod he, 'by Seint Ronyon!　　　　　320
But first,' quod he, 'heere at this alë-stake
I wol both drynke and eten of a cake.'
　And right anon thise gentils gonne to crye;
'Nay, lat hym telle us of no ribaudye!
Telle us some moral thyng, that we may leere　　　　　325
Som wit, and thannë wol we gladly heere.'
　'I graunte, y-wis,' quod he, 'but I moot thynke
Upon som honeste thyng, whil that I drynke.'

Here Folweth The Prologe Of The
Pardoners Tale

　'Lordynges,' quod he, 'in chirchës whan I preche,
I peynë me to han an hauteyn speche,　　　　　　　　330
And rynge it out as round as gooth a belle,
For I kan al by rotë that I telle.
My theme is alwey oon, and evere was,—
Radix malorum est Cupiditas.
　'First, I pronouncë whennës that I come,　　　　　335
And thanne my bullës shewe I, alle and some;
Our ligë lordës seel on my patente,
That shewe I first, my body to warente;
That no man be so boold, ne preest, ne clerk,
Me to distourbe of Cristës hooly werk;　　　　　　　340
And after that thanne telle I forth my tales.

Bullës of popës and of cardynales,
Of patriarkes and bishoppës I shewe,
And in Latyn I speke a wordës fewe
To saffron with my predicacioun,　　　　　　　　　345
And for to stire hem to devocioun.
Thanne shewe I forth my longë cristal stones,
Y-crammëd ful of cloutës and of bones;
Relikes been they, as wenen they echoon;
Thanne have I in latoun a sholder boon　　　　　　350
Which that was an hooly Jewës sheepe.

You, Pardoner, you good fellow,' he said, 'tell us some lighthearted tale or show us some tricks at once.' 'By St Ninian,' replied the Pardoner, 'I shall do that. But,' he continued, 'I must first have a drink and something to eat here at this tavern.'

At once the gentlefolk cried out, 'No, we don't want him to tell us anything ribald. We prefer that he should tell us some edifying story so that we can derive some good sense from it and then we shall willingly listen to him.'

'All right,' he answered, 'I agree to that but I must think up some respectable story while I am having my drink.'

Here Follows The Prologue Of The Pardoner's Tale

'Gentlemen,' the Pardoner began, 'when I preach in church, I take pains to raise my voice and speak in a resonant tone as clear as a bell all the time. Everything I say I know by heart, for my subject is and always has been the same – *Radix malorum est Cupiditas*.

First, I tell them from where I come, then I show every one of my papal bulls and then the King's seal on my papal commission. I show these first to guarantee my personal safety so that neither priest nor cleric dares to interfere with me in Christ's holy work; and then I tell my stories.

I show my bulls issued to me by popes, cardinals, patriarchs and bishops. And I make sure that I say a few words in Latin to give my preachings a tinge of learning and to stir the congregation to devotion. Later I exhibit my long glass flasks, crammed full of rags and bones, which everyone takes to be relics. Again, I have also in a brass box a shoulder bone that was once part of a sheep belonging to a holy Jew.

' "Goode men," I seye, 'taak of my wordës keepe;
If that this boon be wasshe in any welle,
If cow, or calf, or sheepe, or oxë swelle
That any worm hath ete, or worm y-stonge,　　　　　　355
Taak water of that welle and wassh his tonge,
And it is hool anon; and forthermoor,
Of pokkës, and of scabbe, and every soor,
Shal every sheepe be hool that of this welle
Drynketh a draughte. Taak kepe eek what I telle;　　　360
If that the goode-man that the beestës oweth
Wol every wyke, er that the cok hym croweth,
Fastynge, drinkë of this welle a draughte,
As thilkë hooly Jew oure eldrës taughte,
His beestës and his stoor shal multiplie.　　　　　　365

' "And, sires, also it heeleth jalousie;
For though a man be falle in jalous rage,
Lat maken with this water his potage,
And never shal he moore his wyf mystriste,
Though he the soothe of hir defautë wiste,　　　　　370
Al had she taken prestes two or thre.'
' "Here is a miteyn eek, that ye may se!
He that his hand wol putte in this mitayn,
He shal have multiplying of his grayn,
Whan he hath sowën, be it whete or otes,　　　　　375
So that he offrë pens, or ellës grotes.

'Gentlemen,' I declare, 'pay close regard to what I am telling you. If a cow, calf, sheep or an ox which has eaten a worm or has been bitten by a snake, should swell up, provided that this bone has been washed in a well, take water from that well, wash its tongue and the animal will at once be made well. Furthermore, any sheep that drinks from this well will be cured of pocks, scabs and every kind of sore. Now, give your close attention to what I say. If any gentleman who owns cattle will every week, before cock-crow and before he has eaten anything, take a draught from this well, in the same way as the holy Jew instructed our forefathers, both his cattle and farm-stock will multiply.

Further, gentlemen, it also cures jealousy, for, even if a man has fallen into a jealous rage, provided that he makes his stew from this water, he shall never more mistrust his wife, though he was well aware of the evidence of her sin, even if she had taken two or three priests as lovers.

Here too is a glove for you to see. Whoever puts his hand into this glove shall have great increase of the grain he has sown, whether it is wheat or oats, provided that he offers groats or even pence to me.

' "Goode men and wommen, o thyng warne I yow,
If any wight be in this chirchë now
That hath doon synnë horrible, that he
Dar nat for shame of it y-shryven be;   380
Or any womman, be she yong or old,
That hath y-maked hir housbonde cokëwold;
Swich folk shal have no power ne no grace
To offren to my relikes in this place.
And whoso fyndeth hym out of swich blame,   385
They wol come up and offre on Goddës name,
And I assoille hem by the auctoritee
Which that by bulle y-graunted was to me.'
   'By this gaude have I wonnë, yeer by yeer,
An hundred mark sith I was Pardoner.   390
I stondë lyk a clerk in my pulpet,
And when the lewëd peple is doun y-set,
I prechë so, as ye han herd bifoore,
And telle an hundred falsë japës moore.
Thanne peyne I me to strecchë forth the nekke, 395
And Est and West upon the peple I bekke,
As dooth a dowvë sittynge on a berne.
Myne handës and my tongë goon so yerne,
That it is joye to se my bisynesse.
Of avarice and of swich cursednesse   400
Is al my prechyng, for to make hem free
To yeven hir pens, and namely unto me.
For myn entente is nat but for to wynne,
And no thyng for correccioun of synne;
I rekkë neverë whan that they been beryed,   405
Though that hir soulës goon a-blakëberyed.

   Still, good men and women, I warn you of one thing, – if there is now in this church any person who has committed an outrageous sin and dare not, for personal shame, be absolved of it, or any woman, be she young or old, who has deceived and cuckolded her husband. I warn you that such an individual shall have neither the power nor the grace to offer gifts to the relics I have with me here. If anyone considers himself free from such stain, he will approach me and offer gifts in the name of God and I shall grant his absolution by that same authority which has been extended me by the papal bull.

   Ever since I became a Pardoner I have gained a hundred marks every year by means of this trick. I take my stand in my pulpit in the same way as a clergyman does and, when the lay people have sat down, I preach to them in the fashion you have already heard me describe, and then I tell them a hundred more deceitful stories. Now and then I take the trouble to stretch my neck and nod to the congregation in every part, just like a dove does when it is sitting on a barn, at the same time waving my hands and moving my tongue around so briskly that I can assure you it is a delight for anyone to see how hard I have to work. My entire preaching is centred around avarice and wickedness with the sole object of making them generous in offering money, and, of course, especially to me; for my intention is merely to make a profit and is not in any way concerned with the correction of sin. Once a person has been buried in his grave I don't care if his soul does go astray.

For certës many a predicacioun
Comth oftë tyme of yvel entencioun:
Some for pleasaunce of folk and flaterye,
To been avauncëd by ypocrisye: 410
And som for veyne glorie, and some for hate.
For whan I dar noon oother weyes debate,
Thanne wol I stynge hym with my tongë smerte
In prechyng, so that he shal nat asterte
To be defamëd falsly, if that he   415
Hath trespased to my bretheren or to me:
For though I tellë noght his proprë name,
Men shal wel knowë that it is the same
By signës, and by othere circumstances.
Thus quyte I folk that doon us displesances.   420
Thus spitte I out my venym under hewe
Of hoolynesse, to semen hooly and trewe.

'But shortly myn entente I wol devyse,
I preche of no thyng but for coveityse;
Therfore my theme is yet and ever was,   425
Radix malorum est Cupiditas.
Thus kan I preche agayn that samë vice
Which that I use, and that is avarice.
But though myself be gilty in that synne,
Yet kan I maken oother folk to twynne   430
From avarice, and soorë to repente;
But that is nat my principle entente,—
I prechë no thyng but for coveitise:
Of this mateere it oghte ynogh suffise.

I agree that many sermons are inspired by evil intentions – some to please and flatter the congregation, so that hypocrisy can bring the preachers profit, some for sheer boastfulness and others out of spite. When I find no other way to quarrel with an individual I wish to attack, I will then sting them fiercely with my tongue during my sermon, so that, if he has ever offended against any of my order or myself, he will not escape being slandered by me. Even though I do not announce the name of the individual, people can easily recognize from hints and other insinuations I make that he is the person to whom I am referring. In this way I spit out my venom under the guise of holiness, but at the same time I make myself appear pious and devout.

But I must, in a few words, explain my procedure. As I preach on no subject except out of covetousness, my theme has always been – and still is – 'Cupidity is the root of all evil.' As a result, I can preach against the similar vice, avarice, which I myself pursue; for, though I myself am guilty of that sin, yet I can persuade people to abandon avarice and repent very earnestly for their sin.

Still, that is not my principal object. I never preach except out of covetousness; still I have said enough about this matter.

'Thanne telle I hem ensamples many oon   435
Of oldë stories longë tyme agoon;
Fore lewëd peple loven talës olde,
Swiche thyngës kan they wel reporte and holde.
What! trowë ye, the whilës I may preche,
And wynnë gold and silver for I teche,   440
That I wol lyve in poverte wilfully?
Nay, nay, I thoghte it nevere, trewëly.
Fore I wol preche and begge in sondry landes:
I wol nat do no labour with myne handes,
Ne makë baskettës and lyve therby,   445
By cause I wol nat beggen ydelly.

I wol noon of the Apostles countrefete:
I wol have moneie, wollë, chese, and whete,
Al were it yeven of the povereste page,
Or of the povereste wydwe in a village,   450
Al sholde hir children stervë for famyne.
Nay, I wol drynkë licour of the vyne,
And have a joly wenche in every toun.
But herkneth, lordynges, in conclusioun:
Youre likyng is that I shal telle a tale.   455
Now have I dronke a draughte of corny ale,
By God, I hope I shal yow telle a thyng
That shal by resoun been at your likyng;
For though myself be a ful vicious man,
A moral tale yet I yow tellë kan,   460
Which I am wont to prechë, for to wynne.
Now hoold your pees, my tale I wol bigynne.'

Later, I entertain them with many fictitious examples of ancient stories of time long past, because, as you know, uneducated people love old tales which they themselves can remember and repeat to others. What! Do you think that, while I can get gold and silver by my preaching and teaching, I will live in voluntary poverty? No, no, indeed, I would never consider it; for, while I know how to preach and beg in different countries, I will not work with my hands nor make baskets and live on the profits made from that occupation. I am not prepared to go around begging in an idle fashion.

Nor am I prepared to imitate the Apostles. I must have money, wool, cheese and wheat, even though they are given me by the poorest servant or even the poorest widow in a village, whose children might be dying of starvation. No, I must drink the juice of the grape and have a delightful woman in every town. But, gentlemen, pay attention to my concluding remarks. It is your wish that I should tell you a story and, by heaven, now that I have had a draught of this barley-corn beer, I hope that I shall be able to relate to you a story suitable to your taste; for, though I myself am a very wicked man, I can tell you a certain edifying story which I usually narrate to make myself some money. Now, if you will keep quiet, I shall begin my story.'

Heere Bigynneth The Pardoners Tale

In Flaundrës whilom was a compaignye
Of yongë folk, that haunteden folye,
As riot, hasard, stywës, and tavernes, 465
Whereas with harpës, lutës, and gyternes,
They daunce and pleyen at dees, bothe day and nyght,
And eten also, and drynken over hir myght;
Thurgh which they doon the devel sacrifise
Withinne that develes temple, in cursëd wise, 470
By superfluytee abhomynable.
Hir othës been so grete and so dampnable,
That it is grisly for to heere hem swere,
Oure blissëd Lordës body they to-tere:
Hem thoughte that Jewës rente hym noght ynough; 475
And ech of hem at otheres synnë lough.
And right anon thanne comen tombesteres,
Fetys and smale, and yongë frutesteres,
Syngeres with harpës, baudës, wafereres
Whiche been the verray develes officeres, 480
To kyndle and blowe the fyr of lecherye,
That is annexëd unto glotonye.
The Hooly Writ take I to my witnesse,
That luxurie is in wyn and dronkënesse.
Lo, how that dronken Loth, unkindely, 485
Lay by his doghtres two, unwitingly,
So dronke he was, he niste what he wroghte.

Herodës,—whoso wel the stories soghte,—
Whan he of wyn was repleet at his feeste,
Right at his owenë table he yaf his heeste 490
To sleen the Baptist John, ful giltëlees.
Seneca seith a good word, doutëlees;
He seith he kan no differencë fynde
Bitwix a man that it out of his mynde
And a man which that is dronkëlewe, 495
But that woodnessë fallen in a shrewe
Persevereth lenger than dooth dronkenesse.

Here begins the Pardoner's Tale

In Flanders there once lived a company of young men who were given to evil ways, such as debauchery and gambling in brothels and taverns, where they used to dance and play at dice to the accompaniment of harps, lutes and citherns day and night. They also used to eat and drink to excess and, by this means of monstrous excess, they performed sacrifice to the devil in the most wicked fashion in any place of sin.

Their oaths were so outrageously disgusting that it was shocking to hear them swear. They even tore our blessed Lord's body to pieces with their cursing, for it must have seemed to them that the Jews had not torn him apart sufficiently, and, what is more, each of them used to laugh at the other's wickedness. As well as that there used to frequent the places such people as female acrobats, small, agile persons, young fruit-sellers, singers with harps, procurers of women, and cake-sellers, all of whom were fit to be the servants of the devil himself when it came to kindling and blowing up a fire of lechery, a sin closely linked with that of gluttony. I take the Holy Scriptures as my witness that the sin of lechery lies in wine and drunkenness.

See, how the drunken Lot, unnaturally, slept with his two daughters unawares. He was so drunk, he didn't know what he was doing.

If anyone were to search Scriptural history well, he would find that Herod was full of wine at his feast when he gave the order, even at his own table, for John the Baptist to be slain, though he was completely innocent.

Seneca too doubtlessly gives some good advice on this point. He states that he can see no difference between a man who is out of his mind and a man who is habitually drunk except for the fact that, when madness comes to a wicked man, it lasts longer than drunkenness.

   O glotonyë, ful of cursednesse;
O causë first of oure confusioun;
O original of oure dampnacioun,   500
Til Crist hadde boght us with his blood agayn!
Lo, how deerë, shortly for to sayn,
Aboght was thilkë cursëd vileynye:
Corrupt was al this world for glotonye!
Adam oure fader, and his wyf also,   505
Fro Paradys, to labour and to wo
Were dryven for that vice, it is no drede;
For whil that Adam fasted, as I rede,
He was in Paradys; and whan that he
Eet of the fruyt deffended on the tree,   510
Anon he was out cast to wo and peyne.
O glotonye, on thee wel oghte us pleyne!
   O, wiste a man how manye maladyes
Folwen of excesse and of glotonyes,
He woldë been the moorë mesurable   515
Of his dietë, sittynge at his table!
Allas! the shortë throte, the tendrë mouth,
Maketh that Est and West, and North and South,
In erthe, in eir, in water, man to-swynke
To gete a glotoun deyntee mete and drynke.   520
Of this matiere, O Paul, wel kanstow trete!
'Mete unto wombe, and wombe eek unto mete,
Shal God destroyen bothe,' as Paulus seith.
Allas! a foul thyng is it, by my feith,
To seye this word, and fouler is the dede   525
Whan man so drynketh of the white and rede,
That of his throte he maketh his pryvee,
Thurgh thilkë cursëd suprefluitee.

Gluttony is full of wickedness and was the first cause of our shame and the origin of our damnation until Christ redeemed us with his blood! To put it briefly, our wicked conduct has been dearly purchased! All this world grew corrupt with original sin through the gluttony of Adam. There is no doubt but that our father, Adam, and his wife too were driven from Paradise to toil and distress on account of this sin; for, while Adam fasted, so I understand, he remained in Paradise but, as soon as he had eaten the fruit of the forbidden tree, he was straight-away cast out into trouble and misery.

O Gluttony, it well befits us to complain against you! If a man only knew how many maladies result from excess and gluttony, he would be more moderate in his diet at meal-time.

Heaven forbid, the short throat and the tender mouth cause men to labour east and west, north and south, in earth, air and water to provide dainty food and drink for a glutton! You knew, St Paul, how to treat this matter: 'Meats for the belly and the belly too for meats. God shall destroy both it and them,' says Paul. Indeed, I tell you on my word of honour that it is a foul thing to repeat this word but still more wicked is the actual deed when a man has drunk the white and red wine to such excess that, on account of that most wicked excess, he makes his throat a latrine.

The Apostel wepyng seith ful pitously:
'Ther walken manye of whiche yow toold have I,   530
I seye it now, wepyng with pitous voys,
That they been enemys of Cristës croys,
Of whiche the ende is deeth, wombe is hir god.'
O wombe! O bely! O stynking cod!
Fulfilled of donge and corrupcioun!   535
At either ende of thee foul is the soun.

    How greet labour and cost is thee to fynde!
Thise cookës, how they stampe, and streyne, and grynde,
And turnen substaunce into accident,
To fulfillen al thy likerous talent!   540
Out of the hardë bonës knokkë they
The mary, for they castë noght awey
That may go thurgh the golet softe and swoote.

Of spicerie, of leef, and bark, and roote,
Shal been his sauce y-makëd by delit,   545
To make hym yet a newer appetit;
But certës he that haunteth swich delices
Is deed, whil that he lyveth in tho vices.
    A lecherous thyng is wyn, and dronkenesse
Is full of stryvyng and of wrecchednesse.   550
O dronkë man! disfigured is thy face,
Sour is thy breeth, foul artow to embrace,
And thurgh thy dronkë nose semeth the soun,
As though thou seydest ay, 'Sampsoun, Sampsoun!'
And yet, God woot, Sampsoun drank nevere no wyn.
Thou fallest as it were a stykëd swyn;
Thy tonge is lost and al thyn honeste cure;
For dronkenesse is verray sepulture
Of mannës wit and his discrecioun.
In whom that drynke hath dominacioun,   560
He kan no conseil kepe, it is no drede.

The Apostle, weeping most pitifully, says 'For many walk, of whom I have told you often, and now tell you even weeping, that they are the enemies of the cross of Christ, whose end is destruction, whose god is their belly.' O belly! O stomach! You stinking bag! Filled full of dung and rot, the sounds emerging from either end of you are foul. Extreme labour and expense are endured to provide for you. These cooks pound in a mortar, strain through a sieve and grind and change the nature of things completely to satisfy your gluttonous desires so that they may not throw away anything that can go softly and sweetly through the throat.

They even knock the marrow out of hard bones on your behalf. Even a gluttonous man's sauce is deliciously made of spices, leaves, and bark and roots of plants in order to give him a keener appetite. I tell you, a man who practises such pleasures is already dead when he lives among such vices.

Wine is a lustful commodity, while drunkenness is full of strife and wickedness. O drunkard, your face is disfigured, your breath is sour, you are objectionable to embrace, and through your drunken nose you emit a sound as if you were for ever repeating 'Samson! Samson!' And yet, God knows, Samson drank no wine. You stumble around as if you were a stuck pig; your powers of speech and all your regard for decency are lost.

I tell you drunkenness is the very tomb of man's understanding and good sense. Again, there is no doubt but that the person, on whom drink has taken a hold, can keep no secret.

   Now kepe yow fro the white and fro the rede,
And namely fro the whitë wyn of Lepe,
That is to selle in Fysshstrete, or in Chepe.
This wyn of Spaignë crepeth subtilly   565
In othere wynës growynge fastë by,
Of which ther ryseth swich fumositee,
That whan a man hath dronken draughtes thre,
And weneth that he be at hoom in Chepe,
He is in Spaigne, right at the toune of Lepe,   570
Nat at the Rochele, ne at Burdeux toun,
And thannë wol he seye, 'Sampsoun, Sampsoun!'

   But herkneth, lordës, o word, I yow preye,
That alle the sovereyn actës, dar I seye,
Of victories in the Oldë Testament   575
Thurgh verray God that is omnipotent,
Were doon in abstinence and in preyere:
Looketh the Bible and ther ye may it leere.
   Looke, Attilla, the gretë conquerour,
Deyde in his sleepe with shame and dishonour,   580
Bledynge ay at his nose in dronkenesse;
A capitayn sholde lyve in sobrenesse.
And over al this, avyseth yow right wel
What was comaunded unto Lamuel,—
Nat Samuel, but Lamuel seye I;   585
Redeth the Bible, and fynde it expresly
Of wyn-yevyng to hem that han justise.
Namoore of this, for it may wel suffise.

   And now I have yspoke of glotonye,
Now wol I yow deffenden hasardrye.   590
Hasard is verray mooder of lesynges,
And of deceite, and cursëd forswerynges,
Blaspheme of Crist, manslaughtre, and wast also
Of catel, and of tyme; and forthermo
It is repreeve and contrarie of honour   595
For to ben holde a commune hasardour;
And ever the hyer he is of estaat,
The moorë is he holden desolaat.

And so I advise you to abstain from white and red wine, and especially the white wine of Lepe that is being sold in Fish Street or in Cheapside. This Spanish wine is creeping among the other wines that are produced nearby in a cunning way. Further, the drinking of this wine causes very great headiness. Indeed, when a person has consumed three drinks and thinks he is at home in Cheapside, actually he is in the town of Lepe in Spain and not in La Rochelle or Bordeaux. It is when he has drunk this stuff that he will say, 'Samson! Samson!'

But, gentlemen, one further word I beg you. I maintain that all the noble deeds contributed towards victories in the Old Testament, with the help of God who is omnipotent, were performed in abstinence and prayer. If you refer to your Bible, you will learn that there.

Take for example Attila, the renowned conqueror, who died shamefully and dishonourably in his sleep, bleeding continuously from his nose during a bout of drunkenness. A captain should follow a life of sobriety; and, in addition to this, give due consideration to what was commanded Lemuel. (Note, I mean Lemuel, not Samuel.) Read the Bible and you will find it expressly stated there about the giving of wine to people who dispense justice. I shall say no more about this, as I think I have already said enough.

Now that I have spoken about gluttony, I will for your edification forbid gambling. Gambling is the very mother of lies, deceit, wicked perjuries, blaspheming of Christ, manslaughter and also the squandering of goods and time. Furthermore, it is a disgrace and is contrary to personal honour to be considered a public gambler; and the higher the rank the gambler holds, the more abandoned is he considered.

If that a pryncë useth hasardrye,
In allë governaunce and policye   600
He is, as by commune opinioun,
Y-holde the lasse in reputacioun.
    Stilbon, that was a wys embassadour,
Was sent to Corynthe in ful greet honour
Fro Lacidomye to maken hire alliaunce.   605
And when he cam, hym happedë par chaunce
That alle the gretteste that were of that lond
Pleyynge attë hasard he hem fond;
For which, as soonë as it myghtë be,
He stal hym hoom agayn to his contree,   610
And seydë: 'Ther wol I nat lese my name,
Ne I wol nat take on me so greet defame,
Yow for to allie unto none hasardours;

Sendeth otherë wise embassadours,
For, by my trouthë, me were levere dye,   615
Than I yow sholde to hasardours allye;
For ye that been so glorious in honours,
Shul nat allyën yow with hasardours,
As by my wyl, ne as by my tretee!'
This wisë philosophrë thus seyde hee.   620
    Looke eek that to the kyng Demetrius,
The kyng of Parthës, as the book seith us,
Sente him a paire of dees of gold in scorn,
For he hadde usëd hasard ther-biforn;
For which he heeld his glorie or his renoun   625
At no value or reputacioun.
Lordës may fynden oother maner pley
Honeste ynough to dryve the day awey.

If a prince practises dicing, among all governments and politics he is considered by general consent the less worthy in reputation.

When Stilbon, a prudent ambassador, who was sent from Lacedaemon to Corinth in very great honour to make an alliance with the Corinthians, arrived at that city, he happened to find that the principal men of the city were engaged in gambling. As a result, as soon as it could be arranged, he returned once more secretly to his own country and reported to them: 'I am not prepared to lose my reputation at Corinth; nor am I dishonourable as to make an alliance on your behalf with any gamblers.

Send other wise ambassadors, for I would truly prefer to die than make an alliance with gamblers. It is not my personal wish for you, my countrymen who are so glorious in your renown to ally yourselves with gamblers and I shall not make any treaty to that end!' These were the very words this wise philosopher spoke. If you want another example, take the case of King Demetrius. The King of the Parthians, so the story tells us, contemptuously sent him a pair of golden dice, for he had previously been a keen gambler and, as a result, he showed that he set no credit or value to his glory and good name. Gentlemen can find more honourable play of another kind which will make the time pass quickly.

   Now wol I speke of othës false and grete
A word or two, as oldë bookës trete.   630
Gret sweryng is a thyng abhominable,
And fals sweryng is yet moore reprevable.
The heighë God forbad swerying at al:
Witnesse on Mathew; but in special
Of sweryng seith the hooly Jeremye,   635
'Thou shalt seye sooth thyne othës, and nat lye,
And swere in doom, and eek in rightwisnesse';
But ydel sweryng is a cursednesse.
Bihoold and se, that in the firstë table
Of heighë Goddës heestës honurable   640
How that the seconde heeste of hym is this:
'Take nat my name in ydel, or amys.'
Lo, rather he forbedeth swich sweryng
Than homycide, or any cursëd thyng;
I seye that as by ordrë thus it stondeth.   645
This knowen, that his heestës understondeth,
How that the seconde heeste of God is that.
And forther over, I wol thee telle al plat,
That vengeance shal nat parten from his hous
That of his othes is to outrageous:—   650
'By Goddës precious herte!' and, 'By his nayles!'
And 'By the blood of Crist that is in Hayles,
Sevene is my chaunce, and thyn is cynk and treye!'

Now I shall say a few words about severe and false oaths, a subject
that is mentioned in ancient books. Severe swearing is a hateful failing
while false swearing is still more reprehensible. God the omnipotent
forbade swearing in all circumstances and you can refer to St Matthew
for evidence of this; but holy Jeremiah, especially, refers to swearing,
'Thou shall make your oaths truth and never lie; but swear in judgment, and in righteousness.' Pointless swearing, however, is sheer wickedness.

If you take careful note, you will find in the first table of the great God's
honourable commandments that his second commandment is to this
effect: 'Thou shalt not take My name in vain.' Indeed, in an earlier
place, he forbade swearing even before homicide or many other wicked
things – I notice that this is the order in which it stands. Those people
who understand his commandments know very well that this is actually
God's second commandment. Again, I stress quite plainly that vengeance shall not depart from the house of him whose oaths are so
outrageous. 'By the precious heart of God,' 'By his nails,' 'By the blood
of Christ who is in Hales,' 'My chance is seven; yours is five and three.'

'By Goddës armës, if thou falsly pleye,
This daggere shal thurghout thyn hertë go!'—   655
This fruyt cometh of the bicchëd bonës two,
Forsweryng, irë, falseness, homycide.
Now for the love of Crist that for us dyde,
Letë youre othës, bothë grete and smalë.
But, sires, now wol I tellë forth my tale.—   660
    Thise riotourës thre of whiche I telle,
Longe erst er primë rong on any belle,
Were set hem in a taverne for to drynke,
And as they sat they herde a bellë clynke
Biforn a cors was caried to his grave,   665
That oon of hem gan callen to his knave:
'Go bet,' quod he, 'and axë redily
What cors is this that passeth heer forby;
And looke that thou reporte his namë weel,'

    'Sire,' quod this boy, 'it nedeth neveradeel;   670
It was me toold er ye cam heer two houres.
He was, pardee, an old felawe of youres,
And sodeynly he was y-slayn to-nyght
For-dronke, as he sat on his bench upright.
Ther cam a privee theef, men clepeth Deeth,   675
That in this contree al the peplë sleeth,
And with his spere he smoot his herte atwo,
And wente his wey withouten wordës mo.
He hath a thousand slayn this pestilence,
And, maister, er ye come in his presence,   680
Me thynketh that it werë necessarie
For to be war of swich an adversarie;
Beth redy for to meete hym evermoore;
Thus taughtë me my dame; I sey namoore.'

'By the arms of God, if you cheat, this dagger shall pierce through your heart' – the fruit that comes from the cursed pair of dice is perjury, anger, deceit and homicide. Now, please, for the love of Christ who died for us, abandon your oaths, both severe and trivial. Now gentlemen, I shall tell you my story.

Long before any bell rang for the service of prime, these three rioters about whom I have told you were sitting in a tavern to have a drink; and, as they were sitting there, they heard a bell being rung in front of a corpse that was being carried to its burial. One of them called for his servant and ordered him, 'Go quickly and find out at once the name of the dead man who has just been carried past here. See that you report his name speedily to me.'

'Sir,' replied the boy, 'there is no need whatsoever to ask that. I was told his name two hours before you came here and I can assure you he was an old friend of yours, and was suddenly slain last night when he was sitting upright, very drunk, on his bench. A prowling thief, called Death, who is laying low all the people in this country, fell upon him and, with his spear, smote his heart in two and then departed from him in silence.

This plague has already killed a thousand people and so, master, before you approach him, I think it would be well for you to take precautions against such an enemy. From now on be ready to meet him. This is what my mother taught me, so I shall say no more about it.'

'By Seinte Marië!' seyde this taverner,   685
'The child seith sooth, for he hath slayn this yeer,
Henne over a mile, withinne a greet village,
Bothe man and womman, child, and hyne, and page;
I trowe his habitacioun be there.
To been avysëd greet wysdom it were,   690
Er that he dide a man a dishonour.'

'Ye, Goddës armes!' quod this riotour,
'Is it swich peril with hym for to meete?
I shal hym seke by wey and eek by strete,
I make avow to Goddës dignë bones!   695
Herkneth, felawës, we thre been al ones,
Lat ech of us holde up his hand til oother,
And ech of us bicomen otheres brother,
And we wol sleen this falsë traytour, Deeth;
He shal be slayn, which that so manye sleeth,   700
By Goddës dignitee, er it be nyght!'
    Togidres han thise thre hir trouthës plight
To lyve and dyen ech of hem for oother,
As though he were his owene y-borë brother.

And up they stirte, al dronken, in this rage,   705
And forth they goon towardës that village,
Of which the taverner hadde spoke biforn;
And many a grisly ooth thanne han they sworn,
And Cristës blessed body they to-rente,—
Deeth shal be deed, if that they may hym hente.   710
    Whan they han goon nat fully half a mile,
Right as they wolde han troden over a stile,
An oold man and a pourë with hem mette.
This oldë man ful mekëly hem grette,
And seydë thus: 'Now, lordës, God yow see!'   715
    The proudeste of thise riotourës three
Answerde agayn: 'What, carl with sory grace,
Why artow al forwrapped, save thy face?
Why lyvëstow so longe in so greet age?'

'By holy Mary,' exclaimed the tavern-keeper, 'what this lad has said is perfectly true for this plague has slain this year in a large village more than a mile from here both man and woman, child, servant and lad; and I believe that he lives there. It would be very wise for you to take precautions before he does any harm to you.'

'What? By the arms of God,' exclaimed the rioter. 'Is it so dangerous then to meet him? If that is so, I make my vow on the worthy bones of God that I shall seek him out on every road. Listen, friends. The three of us are of one mind so let us give our hands to each other and let each of us become a sworn brother to the other. We shall kill this false traitor, Death, and he who slays so many of our people shall himself be slain, by God's honour, before nightfall.'

Then the three pledged their faith to live and die for each other, just as if he were his own born brother.

They jumped up, though they were quite drunk, in a mad passion and made their way towards the village about which the tavern-keeper had spoken earlier, swearing many blasphemous oaths and tearing to pieces the blessed body of Christ. They vowed that Death would die if they could but catch him.

When they had gone about half a mile and just as they were going to get over a stile, a poor, old man came up to them. This old man greeted them civilly enough and said, 'God bless you, gentlemen!'

The most arrogant of these three rioters addressed him at once. 'What! you fellow, curse you! Why are you completely wrapped up save for your face? Why do you hang on to life to such a great age?'

This oldë man gan looke in his visage,   720
And seyde thus: 'For I ne kan nat fynde
A man, though that I walkëd into Ynde,
Neither in citee, nor in no village,
That woldë chaunge his youthë for myn age;
And therfore moot I han myn agë stille,   725
As longë tyme as it is Goddës wille.
Ne Deeth, allas! ne wol nat han my lyf,
Thus walke I lyk a restëlees kaityf,
And on the ground, which is my moodrës gate,
I knokkë with my staf, erly and late,   730
And seyë: "Leevë mooder, leet me in!
Lo, how I vanysshe, flessh, and blood, and skyn!
Allas! whan shul my bonës been at reste?
Mooder, with yow wolde I chaungë my cheste
That in my chambrë longë tyme hath be,   735
Ye, for an heyrë-clowt to wrappë me!"
But yet to me she wol nat do that grace,
For which ful pale and welkëd is my face.

But, sires, to yow it is no curteisye
To speken to an old man vileynye,   740
But he trespasse in word, or elles in dede.
In Hooly Writ ye may your self wel rede:
"Agayns an oold man, hoor upon his heed,
Ye sholde arise." Wherfore I yeve yow reed,
Ne dooth unto an oold man noon harm now;   745
Namoorë than that ye wolde men did to yow
In agë, if that ye so longe abyde.
And God be with yow, wher ye go or ryde,
I moote go thider as I have to go!"

The old man, looking into his face, answered, 'I live to such a great age because, even though I walk through every city and village as far as India, I just cannot find anyone who is willing to change his youth for my age. And so I must ever keep my old age as long as it is God's will. Alas, Death, too refuses to take my life, and so I am wandering around like a miserable wretch. I am for ever knocking with my staff upon the ground, the gate of Mother Earth, and begging her, "Dear Mother Earth, please allow me to enter! Just look how my flesh, blood and skin are wasting away. Alas, when shall my bones be at rest? Mother, with you I would change my chest that has so long been in my room just for a hair-cloth shroud in which I could wrap myself!" Yet, she will not even do that favour for me, and this anxiety has caused my face to grow deathly pale and wither away.

But, gentlemen, it is discourteous of you to be rude to a man of my years, unless he has done wrong in word or deed to you. You yourselves can read in the Holy Scriptures. 'Thou shalt rise up before the hoary head, and honour the face of an old man,' and so I can offer you this advice. Never do any more harm to an old man than you would like people to do to you when you are old, if, with luck, you live as long as that. May God be with you however you go, as I must now proceeed to the place already determined for me.'

'Nay, oldë cherl, by God, thou shalt nat so!'   750
Seydë this oother hasardour anon;
'Thou partest nat so lightly, by Seint John!
Thou spak right now of thilkë traytour Deeth,
That in this contree alle oure freendës sleeth.
Have heer my trouthe, as thou art his espye,   755
Telle where he is, or thou shalt it abye,
By God and by the Hooly Sacrement!
For soothly thou art oon of his assent
To sleen us yongë folk, thou falsë theef!'
'Now, sires,' quod he, 'if that yow be so leef   760
To fyndë Deeth, turne up this croked wey;
For in that grove I lafte hym, by me fey,
Under a tree, and there he wole abyde;
Noght for youre boost he wole him no thyng hyde.
Se ye that ook? Right there ye shal hym fynde.   765
God savë yow that boghte agayn mankynde,
And yow amende!' thus seyde this oldë man.
And everich of thise riotourës ran
Til he cam to that tree; and ther they founde,
Of floryns fyne of gold y-coynëd rounde,   770
Wel ny an eightë busshels, as hem thoughte.
No lenger thannë after Deeth they soughte,
But ech of hem so glad was of that sighte,
For that the floryns been so faire and brighte,
That doun they sette hem by this precious hoord.   775
The worste of hem he spak the firstë word.

'Oh, no, old peasant, by God, you shall not go away,' said the other gambler at once. 'By Saint John, you are not getting off so lightly! A short time ago you were talking about this traitor, Death, who has been killing all our friends in this country. Take my word for it, by God and by the Holy Sacrament, since we think you are a spy of his and unless you inform us where he is, I promise you shall pay for it. What is more, we are certain that you, you false thief, are one of those who favour his slaying us young people.'

'Now gentlemen,' the old man answered, 'if it is so dear to you to find Death, turn up that winding road; for I give you my word I left him in a grove beneath a tree and I think he is still there. You can boast as much as you like, but he will not hide anything. Can you see that oak-tree? You will find him just there. Now, may God who redeemed mankind bless you and correct your ways!' concluded the old man. All the rioters ran to the tree where they found nearly eight bushels – so they guessed – of fine round florins coined of gold. No longer did they seek for Death but rather all of them were so delighted with this discovery, florins new and shining, that they seated themselves near the precious treasure. Then, the most wicked of them all said:

'Brethren,' quod he, 'taak kepë what I seye;
My wit is greet, though that I bourde and pleye;
This tresor hath Fortune unto us yeven
In myrthe and joliftee our lyf to lyven;   780
And lightly as it comth so wol we spende.
Ey, Goddës precious dignitee! who wende
To-day that we sholde han so fair a grace?
But myghte this gold be caried fro this place
Hoom to myn hous, or ellës unto youres,—   785
For wel ye woot that all this gold is oures,—
Thanne werë we in heigh felicitee!
But trewëly by daye it may nat bee;
Men woldë seyn that we were thevës stronge,
And for oure owenë tresor doon us honge.   790

This tresor moste y-caried be by nyghte
As wisely and as slyly as it myghte.
Wherfor I rede that cut among us alle
Be drawe, and lat se wher the cut wol falle.
And he that hath the cut with hertë blithe   795
Shal rennë to the towne, and that ful swithe,
And brynge us breed and wyn ful privëly;
And two of us shul kepen subtilly
This tresor wel; and if he wol nat tarie,
Whan it is nyght we wol this tresor carie   800
By oon assent, where as us thynketh best.'

'Brothers,' he declared, 'though I jest and fool around, I think I possess a good gift of common sense and so I want you to pay attention to what I am going to say. Fortune has given us this treasure so that we can live a life of carefree gaiety and we shall spend it as easily as we got it. Now, by the precious honour of God, who would have thought this day that we should have such a grand turn of luck? The point is, if this gold could only be carried from here home to my house or even to yours – for you both are now well aware that all this gold is our very own – then we shall be extremely lucky. But we just cannot do it during daylight for people will be sure to say that we are dastardly thieves and would even have us hanged for our own treasure.

Instead, we must carry away the treasure at night-time as prudently and as cunningly as possible; so I advise that lots should be drawn among us to see into whose hands the lot will fall. Then, the fellow who has drawn the lot must hasten very quickly and lightheartedly to the town. From there he must secretly bring us food and drink, while the other two of must keep a careful guard over this treasure. If the one who goes to town does not loiter, we shall carry this treasure, soon as night has fallen, to the place we all consider most suitable.'

That oon of hem the cut broghte in his fest,
And bad hem drawe and looke where it wol falle;
And it fil on the yongeste of hem alle,
And forth toward the toun he wente anon.   805
And al so soonë as that he was gon,
That oon of hem spak thus unto that oother:
'Thow knowest well thou art my swornë brother,
Thy profit wol I tellë thee anon.
Thou woost wel that oure felawe is agon,   810
And heere is gold, and that ful greet plentee,
That shal departed been among us thre.
But nathëlees, if I kan shape it so
That it departed were among us two,
Hadde I nat doon a freendës torn to thee?'   815

    That oother answerde, 'I noot how that may be;
He woot how that the gold is with us tweye;
What shal we doon? what shal we to him seye?'
'Shal it be conseil?' seyde the firstë shrewe,
'And I shal tellen in a wordës fewe   820
What we shal doon, and bryngen it wel aboute.'
'I grauntë,' quod that oother, 'out of doute,
That by my trouthe I shal thee nat biwreye.'
'Now,' quod the firste, 'thou woost wel we be tweye,
And two of us shul strenger be than oon: 825
Looke whan that he is set, and right anoon
Arys, as though thou woldest with hym pleye,
And I shal ryve hym thurgh the sydës tweye,
Whil that thou strogelest with hym as in game;

And with thy daggere looke thou do the same;   830
And thanne shal al this gold departed be,
My deerë freend, bitwixen me and thee,
Thanne may we both our lustës all fulfille,
And pleye at dees right at oure owenë wille.'
And thus accorded been thise shrewës tweye,   835
To sleen the thridde, as ye han herd me seye.

The speaker then brought the lots in his fist and bade the others draw to see on whom the lot would fall. It so happened that the lot fell upon the youngest of them and he at once made his way towards the town. No sooner had he gone than one of the other two said to the other: 'You know you are my sworn brother, so I intend telling you something which will be to your advantage. You see that our friend has just gone and left the gold with us — and that in sufficient quantity to be split between the three of us. But all the same if I can arrange it so that it was divided between us two, wouldn't I have done you a good turn?'

'I don't see how that can be done,' replied the second rioter. 'Our mate knows very well that we two have the gold with us so what can we do about it? What can we say to him?'

'Well, if you promise to keep it a secret,' said the other, 'I shall quite briefly explain to you what we can do to bring it about successfully.'

'I quite agree to that,' said the second rascal, 'and I promise on my honour I shall not betray you.'

'Now,' said the first rioter, 'you are aware that there are two of us and, of course, two are stronger than one. When he returns watch for him to sit down and then get up at once as if you wanted to play with him; and, while you are struggling as if in fun with him, I shall run him through.

At the same time you must do the same as I with your dagger. Then all this gold can be shared, my dear friend, between you and me. In this way we can both fulfil our desires and play at dice to our hearts' content.' This then was the agreement made between these two rascals, to slay the third member, as I have outlined to you.

This yongeste, which that wente unto the toun,
Ful ofte in herte he rolleth up and doun
The beautee of thise floryns newe and brighte.
'O Lord,' quod he, 'if so were that I myghte   840
Have al this tresor to my selfe allone,
Ther is no man that lyveth under the trone
Of God, that sholdë lyve so murye as I!'
And attë laste the feend, oure enemy,
Putte in his thought that he sholde poyson beye,   845
With which he myghtë sleen hise felawes tweye;
For why the feend foond hym in swich lyvynge
That he hadde levë hym to sorwë brynge;
For this was outrëly his fulle entente
To sleen hem bothe, and nevere to repente.   850
     And forth he gooth, no lenger wolde he tarie,
Into the toun, unto a pothecarie,
And preydë hym that he hym woldë selle
Som poyson, that he myghte his rattës quelle:
And eek ther was a polcat in his hawe,   855
That, as he seyde, his capouns hadde y-slawe;
And fayn he woldë wreke hym, if he myghte,
On vermyn, that destroyëd hym by nyghte.

The pothecarie answerde: 'And thou shalt have
A thyng that, al so God my soulë save,   860
In al this world ther is no creature,
That eten or dronke hath of this confiture,
Noght but the montance of a corn of whete,
That he ne shal his lif anon forlete;
Ye, sterve he shal, and that in lassë while   865
Than thou wolt goon a-paas nat but a mile;
This poyson is so strong and violent.'
     This cursëd man hath in his hond y-hent
This poyson in a box, and sith he ran
Into the nextë strete unto a man,   870
And borwëd of hym largë botelës thre,
And in the two his poyson poured he.

In the meantime the youngest who had made his way towards the town kept meditating in his heart on the beauty of the new, shining florins. 'O Lord,' he said to himself, 'if it could only come about that I could have all this treasure for myself alone there is no one under the heavens who could live as happily as I!'

In the end, the devil, our enemy, finding him to be in a suitable frame of mind, whereby he knew he could work mischief for him, put the thought into his head that he should buy poison with which he could kill his two companions. It was clearly his full intention to kill the both of them without feeling any compunction for the deed.

He no longer loitered but went on his way to the town. He called in a chemist's and asked if he would sell him some poison to kill rats in his house and a polecat which roamed his yard as well and had, so he claimed, even killed his fowls. He very much desired, he said, to destroy this vermin if possible that disturbed him at night.

'God bless my soul!' the chemist said. 'You shall have something which will immediately kill any animal in the whole world that eats or drinks no more of this preparation than is equal to the amount of a grain of wheat. Yes, this poison is so strong and violent that it will destroy in less time than you would take to walk a mile at an easy pace.'

The wicked man seized the poison box in his hands and then ran to the nearest street to see another man from whom he borrowed three large bottles for himself and in two of the bottles he poured his poison.

The thridde he kepte clene for his owenë drynke,
For al the nyght he shoope him for to swynke
In cariynge of the gold out of that place.   875
And when this riotour with sory grace
Hadde filled with wyn his gretë botels thre,
To his felawes agayn repaireth he.
    What nedeth it to sermone of it moore?
For right as they hadde cast his deeth bifoore,   880
Right so they han hym slayn, and that anon.
And whan that this was doon, thus spak that oon:
'Now lat us sitte and drynke, and make us merie,
And afterward we wol his body berie';
And with that word it happëd hym par cas,   885
To take the botel ther the poysoun was,
And drank, and yaf his felawe drynke also,
For which anon they storven bothë two.
    But certës, I suppose that Avycen
Wroot nevere in no Canon, ne in no Fen,   890
Mo wonder signës of empoisonyng
Than hadde thise wrecches two er hir endyng.
Thus ended been thise homycidës two,
And eek the false empoysonere also.

    O cursëd synne of allë cursednesse!   895
O traytours homycide, O wikkednesse!
O glotonye, luxurie, and hasardrye!
Thou blasphemour of Crist with vileynye,
And othës grete, of usage and of pride!
Allas! mankyndë, how may it bitide   900
That to thy Crëatour, which that thee wroghte,
And with his precious hertë-blood thee boghte,
Thou art so fals and so unkynde, allas!

The third he kept clean for his own drink (for he intended to work hard all that night in order to carry the gold from that place). After this the rioter, with evil intention, filled his three large bottles with wine and returned once more to his friends.

Why should I make a long sermon about it? Just as they had planned his death beforehand, so they quickly killed him and, after it was done, one of them said: 'Now then, let us sit down and have a drink and enjoy ourselves. After that we shall bury his body.'

On these words it chanced that he took the bottle with the poison, drank from it and then gave it to his companion to have a drink as well. Of course, the two of them died on the spot.

Indeed, I am certain that Avicenna never described in any part of his 'Canon Medicinae' more strange symptoms of poisoning than these two wretches displayed before their death. In this way these two murderers and the false poisoner as well met their end.

O most wicked sin of wickedness! O traitorous homicide! O wickedness! O gluttony, lust and gambling! You who blaspheme Christ with your outrageous conduct, severe oaths, instigated both from habit and violence of character! Indeed, my fellow-men, how can it come about that you are so false and hard-hearted to your Creator who made you and redeemed you with the precious blood of his heart!

Now, goode men, God foryeve yow youre trespas,
And ware yow fro the synne of avarice! 905
Myn hooly pardoun may yow alle warice,
So that ye offre nobles, or sterlynges,
Or ellës silver broches, spoonës, rynges.
Boweth youre heed under this hooly bulle!
Com up, ye wyvës, offreth of youre wolle! 910
Youre names I entre heer in my rolle anon,
Into the blisse of hevene shul ye gon;
I yow assoillë by myn heigh powër,
Yow that wol offre, as clene and eek as cleer
As ye were born; and lo, sires, thus I preche! 915
And Jhesu Crist, that is oure soulës leche,
So grauntë you his pardoun to receyve,
For that is best, I wol yow nat deceyve!

'But, sires, o word forgat I in my tale:
I have relikes and pardoun in my male 920
As faire as any man in Engelond,
Whiche were me yeven by the Popës hond.

If any of yow wole of devocioun
Offren, and han myn absolucioun,
Com forth anon, and kneleth heere adoun, 925
And mekëly receyveth my pardoun;
Or ellës, taketh pardoun as ye wende,
Al newe and fressh at every milës ende,
So that ye offren, alway newe and newe,
Nobles or pens, whiche that be goode and trewe. 930
It is an honour to everich that is heer
That ye mowe have a suffisant Pardoneer
Tassoillë yow in contree as ye ryde,
For aventures whiche that may bityde.
Paraventure ther may fallen oon or two 935
Doun of his hors, and breke his nekke atwo;
Looke which a seuretee is it to yow alle,
That I am in youre felaweshipe y-falle.

Now, gentlemen, may God forgive you your sins and protect you from the sin of avarice. My sacred indulgences can save you all provided you offer me gold and silver coins, or even brooches, spoons or rings. Bow your heads to this papal bull! Approach, you women, and give me of your wool; after that, I shall immediately enter your names on my roll that I have here with me. Then you too will enter the bliss of heaven. By my great power I shall absolve you who offer gifts as cleanly and as purely as when you were born. Yes, gentlemen, this is my method of preaching and may Jesus Christ, the healer of our souls, allow you to receive his pardon; for that is the best of all – I do not wish to deceive you.

But, gentlemen, I forgot one thing in my story. I have relics and indulgences in my bag and they are as good as any man has in England, and they were granted me by the Pope's authority.

If any of you wish, out of piety, to offer gifts and receive my absolution, come forward at once, kneel down here and meekly receive my forgiveness. Otherwise, you can seek forgiveness during our journey, quite fresh and prompt, at the end of every mile we travel – provided, of course, that you offer me gold coins or pence which are good and genuine every time. It is an honour for every one of you present that you are accompanied by a Pardoner who is able to absolve you during your journey against any accidents which may happen. Perhaps one or two of you may fall from his horse and break his neck in two. See what a blessing it is to you all that I have joined your company.

That may assoillë yow, bothe moore and lasse,
Whan that the soule shal fro the body passe.   940
I redë that oure Hoost heere shal bigynne,
For he is moost envoluped in synne!
Com forth, sire Hoost, and offrë first anon,
And thou shalt kisse my relikes everychon,
Ye, for a grote! Unbokele anon thy purs!'   945
    'Nay, nay,' quod he, 'thanne have I Cristës curs!
Lat be,' quod he, 'it shal nat be, so theech!
Thou woldest make me kisse thyn oldë breech,
And swere it were a relyk of a seint.
Though it were with thy fundement depeint!   950
But by the croys which that seint Eleyne fond,
I wolde I hadde thy coillons in my hond
In stide of relikes or of seintuarie.
Lat kutte hem of, I wol thee helpe hem carie;
They shul be shrined in an hogges toord!'

    This Pardoner answerdë nat a word,
So wrooth he was: no word ne wolde he seye.

    'Now,' quod oure Hoost, 'I wol no lenger pleye
With thee, ne with noon oother angry man.'
But right anon the worthy Knyght bigan,   960
Whan that he saugh that al the peple lough:—
    'Namoore of this, for it is right ynough!
Sire Pardoner, be glad and myrie of cheere,
And ye, sir Hoost, that been to me so deere,
I prey yow that ye kisse the Pardoner!   965
And Pardoner, I prey thee drawe thee neer,
And as we diden, lat us laughe and pleye!'
Anon they kiste and ryden forth hir weye.

Heere is Ended The Pardoners Tale

I can absolve you, both high and low, if the soul should depart from the body. I advise you that our Host here with us shall be first, as he is the most enveloped in sin. Come forward, sir Host, and be the first to offer gifts – then you may kiss every one of the relics, even for a groat. Come on, open up your purse!'

'No, no,' the Host answered. 'May I have Christ's curse upon me if I do. Leave me alone,' he went on. 'So may I thrive I am not interested. You would make me kiss your old breeches and swear they were the relics of a saint, even if they were smeared with your dung. By the cross which Saint Helena found, don't I wish I had your testicles in my hand instead of relics or a casket. Let them be cut off, I will help you carry them – they shall be enshrined in a pig's turd!

The Pardoner was so angry that he would not utter a word.

'Now,' said our Host, 'I will not fool any longer with you nor with any other angry person.' When the noble Knight saw that all the people were laughing, he at once said, 'Stop this; it is quite enough! Sir Pardoner, cheer up and put on a bright face. And you, Sir Host who are so dear to me, I beg you kiss the Pardoner. And, Pardoner, I beg you come nearer and then, as we did before, let us laugh and be merry.' They kissed each other at once and rode forward on their way.

The Pardoner's Tale ends here

Textual notes

The character of the Pardoner

Line 669 Chaucer has just told us something of the Summoner, obviously a disreputable character; the Pardoner is introduced as his friend and comrade, singing in a high-pitched voice some popular and possibly ribald song of the time, the words quoted being 'Come hider, Love, to me'; the deep trumpet-tones of the Summoner were his accompaniment.

670 **Rouncival** A 'cell' of the Priory of Our Lady of Roncesvalles, in the Pyrenees, had been established near Charing Cross. The modern Hospital is probably a relic of the foundation.

671 **Rome** The word is a dissyllable. At the time at which Chaucer wrote, there were rival Popes, at Rome and at Avignon (1378–1417). England sided with the Pope at Rome.

677 **ounces** Clusters, dribblets, bunches, coils (like Sir Andrew's in *Twelfth Night*, perhaps).

680 **for jolitee** For pleasure. He was on holiday, and enjoying himself.

682 **the newe jet** The latest fashion.

683 **dischevele** With hair untidy.

685 **vernicle** St Veronica, according to legend, lent her kerchief to Christ to wipe His face as He carried His cross to Calvary. When He returned it, it bore the imprint of His face. A vernicle is a copy of this portrait.

687 The frivolous phrasing of this line suggests something of Chaucer's attitude to the question of Pardons and their sale.

692 **Berwyk unto Ware** Roughly, from one end of England to the other.

695 **Oure Lady veyl** There was in Old English no inflexion to the word 'lady' to mark the genitive case.

699 **latoun** A kind of brass. The stones would be some sort of semi-precious ornament on the cross.

701 The word 'relikes' might well appear between inverted commas.

702 **person** Parson.

up on lond Up country, in a remote part.

703 **him** Himself, i.e. the Pardoner.

705 **japes** Tricks, foolish tales, forms of deception.

706 **made . . . his apes** Made them his dupes, deceived them.

707 atte laste To sum up.

708 ecclesiaste Preacher.

noble Probably used ironically.

709 lessoun A passage from the Scriptures or from the writings of the Church Fathers.

storie The legend, or life, of a Saint.

710 offertorie During the service of the Mass, the people presented their offerings, formerly of bread and wine, but later of money. The Pardoner sang during this collection, which was for the benefit of the church in which he had spoken. The sale of Pardons was a separate ceremony.

alderbest Best of all.

712 affyle Make smooth – in two senses.

The Words of the Host to the Doctor and the Pardoner

Line 287 The Doctor had spoken about one Appius Claudius who had bribed a churl to swear that a certain girl, Virginia, had been stolen while she was that churl's. When the case came before Appius, the 'fals justise', he ordered her to be handed over to his own keeping pending her being restored to her supposed master. Realizing the fate in store for her, her own father, Virginius, slew her. Greatly moved by the story, the Host, Harry Bailly, gave vent to his feelings.

gan to swere Began to swear (**gan swere**, without the 'to', would be the past tense: 'swore'.) **'gan to'** suggests more than a momentary outburst.

288 harrow A cry of distressed astonishment – 'Heaven help us!'

nayles Almost certainly a reference is to the nails which fastened Our Lord to the Cross. (See also line 651.)

Blood The blood of Christ.

291 thise Of this kind.

292 sely Innocent. This word, which earlier still had meant 'blessed', did not receive its meaning 'silly', 'foolish' till about 1550.

293 deere Frequently, as here, the final -*e* indicates an adverb.

boughte Paid for.

295 The gift of Fortune is wealth; the gift of Nature is beauty.

300 men Used impersonally. Translate, here and elsewhere, by 'we', or 'anyone'.

301 The reference is to the Doctor.

302 pitous Pitiful.

303 passe over Let us drop the subject.

is no fors It does not matter.

306 Medical vessels and bottles. The Host was an ignorant man, and probably quite unable to grasp the meaning of unusual words. **Hippocrates** is the Greek 'Father of medicine', living about the fifth century BC. There was a spiced wine '**ypocras**' which the Host would know about: he seems to have confused the two. In the same way, **Galen,** of the second century AD, may be confused here with **gallons**. At any rate, the precise meaning of the line escapes us.

307 letuarie A medicinal preparation, a powder enclosed in honey.

309 so moot I theen So may I prosper. This phrase, frequently found in Chaucer, may be translated by 'upon my life'.

propre Fine-looking.

310 The well-built monk of the Prologue was said to be 'fit to be an abbot'.

Seint Ronyan Some of the Chaucer manuscripts have 'Seint Ninyan', to whom Bede refers. It is difficult to explain why the Host refers to either saint. It has been suggested that he invented the name, which happened to be that of a real saint by coincidence. The Host says he 'cannot speak in set phrases', and this line may offer an example of his inability to use right words.

312 'makest my heart grieve' He is still thinking of Virginia's fate.

313 cardynacle A mistake for cardiacle, meaning heartburn.

314 By corpus bones Another of the Host's mistakes, for the words have no meaning. Translate, if at all, by 'the body and bones of Christ'.

but Unless.

triacle Really, an antidote for poison; here, a restorative.

315 moyste Freshly brewed.

corny Full of substance, tasting strongly of malt.

318 He turns from the Doctor and sees the Pardoner, whom he addresses as 'my good friend'.

319 myrthe Something jolly.

japes Jests, idle tales.

anon At once.

320 The Pardoner adopts the Host's newly-found Saint.

321 ale-stake By luck they were actually passing a tavern where the restorative could be obtained. An ale-stake was a horizontal pole to which a bunch of greenery had been tied, as an indication that ale could be had inside the house.

322 cake A small loaf of bread, not sweetened at all.

323 thise An emphatic word, used like the Latin 'ille'. 'These well-bred fellow-travellers of ours' were afraid of what the Pardoner might tell them. Having been for some time with him on the road to Canterbury,

they demanded something worthy of their intelligence. The Pardoner
is ready to meet their wishes but asks for their indulgence while he
thinks of something suitable.

328 **honeste** Respectable, worthy of the company, which included at
least three ladies, of whom one, it must be said, was very
broadminded.

The Prologue of the Pardoner's Tale

Line 329 Before telling the 'honest' thing he has thought of while in
the alehouse, the Pardoner gives the pilgrims some idea of his pulpit
manner, and of the matter of his address.

Lordynges Gentlemen. Again he does not mention the presence of the
ladies.

330 **hauteyn** Loud. Line 688 tells us he had a voice 'as smal as hath a
goot'. Bell-like tones suggested by 'hauteyn' would be difficult for him
to produce. We shall find throughout the Tale that his statements
cannot be relied upon.

speche Voice.

332 He would seem to be a man of one speech, continually repeated. It
should be remembered that we are not told that he was a cleric; he
may well have been a layman.

334 'Love of money is the root of all evil'. Timothy, 6,10. In the *Parson's
Tale* Chaucer translates the Latin by 'the rote of alle harmes is
coveitise.'

335 He had just come with a wallet 'bret-ful of pardon come from Rome
al hoot'.

336 **bulles** Literally, leaden seals attached to documents, to prove their
authenticity. He details them in lines 337, 342, and 343.

alle and some One and all.

337 **our lige lord** Most probably the King of England, Richard II.
Some think the reference is to the Pope. The **patente** would be a letter
addressed to anyone whom it might concern authorizing the presence
and the activities of the Pardoner. The word 'patent' means 'open for
all to read'.

339 A clerk might be a cleric or a layman.

340 **distourbe** Drive away from.

341 **tales** Such, for example, as those found in lines 352–374.

342 After the reference in line 341 to 'tales' we may suspect that these
bulls were false.

343 **patriarkes** Heads of groups of Archbishops.

345 'To flavour my preaching with'. The few Latin words would suggest to the ignorant laity that the speaker was a learned man.

347 **longe cristal stones** Probably glass flasks or bottles.

348 **cloutes** Pieces of cloth. Refer to 695–700.

351 We have no clue to the identity of this '**holy jew**'. In lines 364–5 the reference may be to Jacob. See Genesis 30,31–43.

353–6 The syntax is confused. If we understand the word 'then' before line 354, the meaning becomes clearer. The bone gives magic properties to the water in which it is washed.

355 'Which has eaten a snake, or which a snake has stung'.

361 **goode-man** Master, householder.

oweth Owns.

362 **hym** This is usually called an 'ethic' dative: 'crows for him', that is to waken him.

364 **thilke** This same. See line 351.

365 **stoor** Grain, as opposed to animals or other livestock.

368 **lat maken . . . his potage** Let his broth be made – presumably by his wife. The 'men' of line 352 refers to people generally.

369 **mystriste** Suspect.

defaute Wrongdoing.

372 **mitayn** Mitten. A glove of this sort was commonly worn when corn was being sown.

376 There is a condition to be fulfilled before these marvels can be expected to materialize.

379 **horrible** Outrageous. Our word 'horrible' is too mild to translate Chaucer's thought.

380 'That for very shame he dare not confess it'.

382 'Been unfaithful to her husband'.

385 **out of** Free from.

blame Imputation.

hym himself.

387 **assoille** absolve.

388 **Bulle** The Pope's bull.

389 Having ended the verbatim account of his method of cajoling the poor to part with their pence or groats, the Pardoner confesses that he has no interest in their well-being, and continues an account of his performance in the pulpit.

gaude Trick, trickery.

390 **an hundred mark** A mark was worth two-thirds of a pound. An

up-country clergyman might receive as much as £5 a year in those times, and a comparison between what is gained by an honest man and the takings of this fraudulent Pardoner suggests something of the wages of his deceit.

391 **lyk** As if I were a regular clergyman.

pulpet The pulpit in the Middle Ages was roughly half-way down the nave. The preacher stood with his back to the wall, facing north or south. He would thus have to turn east and west in turn to include all members of the congregation, who sat on the floor on rushes.

394 **an hundred** Doubtless meaning 'very many'.

395 **peyne me** Exert myself, take pains.

396 **bekke** Nod, imitate the action of a pigeon on a barn-roof.

398 **yerne** Quickly, readily; glibly.

399 'It is a joy to see how busy I am'.

400 **avarice and swich cursednesse** In other words, 'cupiditas', line 334.

403 'My purpose is only for my personal gain.'

404 **no thyng** Not at all.

405–6 The general sense is that he doesn't care what happens to their souls when they're dead.

to goon blakeberyed Pass the time picking blackberries. All the Pardoner wants is their money.

407–8 'Many a fine sermon is preached with evil intention.' The following lines illustrate his comment.

412 **debate** Quarrel. If he is too timid to quarrel openly, he can injure his enemy by words from the pulpit.

414 **asterte** Escape, avoid. The security of the pulpit is used to take away his enemy's character falsely. If the Pardoner owes him a grudge, the Pardoner is so cowardly as to refrain from naming his victim. By some kind of hidden reference, or by pointing at him, he singles out the man he is attacking.

421 **hewe** Countenance, pretence, colour.

422 So as to seem holy and truthful.

423 **devyse** Explain.

424 **for coveityse** Because of covetousness, because I am covetous. (See lines 427–31.)

427 In this way I can preach against the same vice as I practise.

432 If he makes a convert from greed, his success is quite accidental. He does not preach to convict of sin.

435 **ensamples** Illustrations of the theme of the effects of

covetousness. Several books of such **exempla** were current in the middle ages.

438 reporte and holde Repeat to their friends and keep in their memory.

439 what! Possibly the reply of the Pardoner to an interruption from the audience.

440 for I teche As the result of my teaching.

441 wilfully Of my own free will.

442 I thoght it nevere It never came into my mind.

446 'Because I do not beg without gaining some profit for myself.'

447 countrefete Imitate. The apostles were instructed to depend on the hospitality of those to whom they spoke. See St Mark, 6,7,10.

448 The reference to wool, the staple product of the kingdom at this time, is significant.

451 sterve Die. The Prologue to the *Canterbury Tales* has a reference to this grasping characteristic of the Pardoner. We should notice that he boasts of his extortion even from the very poor.

455 your likyng is It is your wish.

458 by resoun Reasonably.

at your likyng Suit your desires.

The Pardoner's Tale

Line 463 The Tale which follows is first found in a Persian poem of the twelfth century. There is also an Arabic version, which possibly had been brought to Europe by returning Crusaders, for it also appears in an Italian setting. It is owing to the genius of Chaucer that the Pardoner places the incidents in Flanders, a country which was well-known to Englishmen who travelled in connection with the wool trade, and whose natives were frequently to the fore in England itself. Had the Tale been placed in a remote country, its application would have been less immediate; Englishmen knew Flemings; it was to three of their compatriots that these untoward events occurred.

464 haunteden Practised. The Wife of Bath had a 'haunt' of cloth-making. 'gave themselves up to' gives the idea of the meaning.

folye All kinds of folly.

465 as Such as.

riot Dissolute living.

hasard Gambling.

stywes Brothels. **Hasard** is also the name of a game played with dice. See line 608.

466 These are all stringed instruments. **Gyternes** are citterns or guitars.

468 over hir myght To excess.

469 thurgh which Whereby.

devel Dative case.

470 in cursed wise In wicked fashion.

471 superfluytee Excesses.

474 to-tere Tear to pieces. The particle **to-** has an intensive force. The reference is to such phrases as are found in lines 692, 695. The idea is repeated by the use of the word **to-rente**, in 609.

477 tombesteres Acrobats, dancing girls. In the southern dialects of Old English, **-estere** was a characteristic feminine ending. It is preserved in certain words, now no longer feminine, used as occupational names, e.g. Baxter, a female baker; Webster, a female weaver; Spinster, which retains its feminine significance, meant a female spinner. But all words with this termination were not originally feminine; such are **songster** and **youngster**.

478 frutesteres Fruit women.

wafereres Sellers of wafers, or thin cakes.

480 whiche Who (*not* which).

verray Veritable.

officers Agents.

481 blowe . . . lecherye Fan the flame of lust.

annexed Bound up with.

484 There is wantonness in wine and intemperance.

486 niste Knew not (**ne+wiste**). Similarly, **nis** for **ne+wis**; **noot** for **ne+woot**.

488 As we should expect, there are many references to incidents recorded in the Bible or evils resulting from excessive drinking and eating. Here follow illustrations from the life of Herod, and Adam and Eve, to be supplemented from a secular tradition about Attila. The reference to Herod, line 488, is obscure.

'who so . . . soghte' might be rendered 'who so thoroughly sought the records', in which case the Pardoner would be thinking of Herod's command to the Wise Men to search through the traditions about the King who was to be born, as mentioned in St Matthew, 2,7. On the other hand, the translation might be parenthetical; 'whoever has sought the records well (will remember this') and refer to the fact that a student of Scripture would recall the account of the murder of St John the Baptist.

491 ful gilteless Who was quite innocent of the crime of which he was accused.

492 **Senec** Seneca, who died in 65 AD was one of the tutors of Nero. He wrote many works of moral philosophy. The reference in this passage is to one of his letters.

495 **dronkelewe** Addicted to drunkenness. The suffix **-lewe** is not infrequent in Chaucer's period and means 'characterized by'.

496 **woodnesse** Madness.

shrewe In Elizabethan times the word referred to a scolding woman.

in a shrewe Upon a rascal.

498 Apostrophes beginning with the interjection 'O'! are characteristic of the Pardoner's oratory. See lines 512, 513, 521, 534 etc.

499 **confusion** Downfall, ruin.

501 **boght . . . agayn** Redeemed.

502 **deere** At what a high price.

507 **it is no drede** There is no doubt. This phrase is very common in Chaucer; sometimes it seems to have no definite meaning, and is used to provide a rhyme, or even to fill up the decasyllabic line.

510 **deffended** Forbidden. The word has the same meaning as its French counterpart today. The meaning changed in English almost entirely; to defend a practice means the opposite of to forbid it.

eet Ate.

511 **anon** Immediately.

wo and peyne Sorrow and suffering.

512 **on thee . . . pleyne** With good reason ought we to complain about you.

513 **wiste** Conditional; 'if a man knew . . .'

515 **mesurable** Restrained, moderate. Chaucer uses this word of the Doctor. Line 435.

517 **tendre** Sensitive, delicate. The reference is to the palate.

518 **maketh that** Is the cause that, brings it about that . . .

519 **in erthe** To provide meats, and possibly vegetables; in air for fowl.

In water For fish.

520 **deyntee** Rare.

521 **kanstow** Canst thou, didst thou.

522 'The food for the belly, and the belly for the food', 1 Corinthians, 6,13.

524 It is dreadful indeed to mention this text.

526 **so** In such a way, to such an extent.

white and red These were imported from France by such as the Shipman of the *General Prologue*. Lines 388–410.

527 The drinker takes so much wine that he hardly tastes it; it is much as if he poured it down a drain.

529 **wepyng** In tears. (Philippians, 3,18).

534 'O stomach, O belly, O stinking bag!'

535 **fulfilled** Filled full.

537 **fynde** To provide for you. 'All found' used to be part of the advertisements for domestic helpers; it meant 'everything provided'.

538 **stampe** Pound the foods.

streyne Strain through the sieve.

539 Changes the very nature of the ingredients. The original appearance of the ingredients – their nature – was transformed into something quite different. The nature was changed into something quite other in appearance.

540 **talent** Gluttonous desire.

545 **by delyt** Daintily, to give delight.

546 **a newer appetit** An appetite for a new flavour.

547 **haunteth** Practises such delights.

548 **lyveth in** devotes himself to.

550 **is ful of** Is allied to, brings with it.

stryvyng Contention.

553 The sound through your drunken nose seems as if you were saying 'Samson' all the time. The snoring of a drunken man might possibly sound like those two syllables.

555 The Pardoner was certainly not ignorant of the words of the Scriptures. Samson was a Nazarite, and as such would not take wine.

556 **fallest** Tumble about.

styked swyn A stuck pig.

557 'Your tongue is useless and you have no concern for honourable things.'

558 'Is indeed the grave of a man's intelligence and power of understanding.'

560 'A man overcome by drink can keep no secrets, indeed.'

563 **the white wyn of Lepe** The white wine of Lepe in NW Spain, was evidently heavy, and was used to adulterate other wines. See line 565.

564 **to selle** To be sold, to be bought.

Fysshstrete Is near the famous Billingsgate Fish Market and Chepe is now Cheapside, the word meaning a market. As Chaucer's father had a vintner's business near Fish Street, we are not surprised to find his son with a knowledge of some of the tricks of the trade, though he sets his knowledge before us in a facetious manner. It is the heavy Spanish wine which creeps into vineyards of Gascony; Chaucer does not even hint at any human agent in the adulteration.

568 The wine of Lepe overcomes the choicer wines of La Rochelle and

Bordeaux; after three draughts the tippler finds himself carried away to Lepe, and is heard to be snoring to the words 'Samson, Samson'.

573 The Pardoner, after a reference to the Old Testament, passes on to an anecdote of Attilla and closes this section on gluttony with a final exhortation to his hearers to 'redeth the Bible!'

573 **herkneth** Listen to. The verb is transitive in Middle English usage.

574 **sovereyn** Chief, noble

actes Chronicles, reports

576 **thurgh** Through the might of.

verray True. We still sometimes use the word 'very' in the sense of 'true'.

578 **looketh** Search (imperative plural).

leere Learn. But not many of those on the pilgrimage could read at all, let alone the Latin into which the Bible had been translated by Jerome.

579 Attila, a world conqueror, whose conquests extended to the Great Wall of China, was first checked at the battle of Chalons in 451. He died on the night of his marriage to a German girl, who is accused of murdering him. Chaucer adopts another account, that he died through the bursting of a blood vessel.

583 **avyseth yow** Consider. The 'yow' is a reflective object which we cannot easily translate. The line means: 'and in addition to this, ponder in your mind what was commanded to Lamuel' (Proverbs, 31,4).

585 The audience would naturally think he had mentioned the far better known Biblical character, Samuel the prophet. Lamuel, also called Lemuel, is the reputed author of the last chapter of the Book of Proverbs, in which kings are exhorted to be temperate for the sake of their subjects.

586 **redeth, fynde** Both are imperative plurals. The form 'fyndeth' would make the line too long: as it is, the final -e is elided before the vowel in 'it'.

expresly Distinctly. We must understand such an idea as 'stated' after this word.

587 **of wyn-yevyng** About the giving of wine.

han justise Dispense justice, administer the law.

588 At this point the Pardoner ends his attack on gluttony, and takes up the subject of gambling.

590 **deffenden** Forbid, not defend. **Yow** is a dative, called the 'ethic' dative by grammarians. It means 'for your benefit' or 'in your presence' not 'I must forbid you to gamble'.

591 Lies, cheating, perjury, blasphemy, manslaughter, waste of time, and property may all be the result of gambling. To be reputed a public

gambler is a disgrace and the contrary to one's personal honour, and the higher the rank of the gambler, the more abandoned is he considered to be.

599 **useth hasardrye** Makes a habit of gambling. In translating these few lines, let line 600 be the last in the paragraph.

603 **Stilbon** This anecdote, and that concerning King Demetrius, line 621, are found in the Polycraticus written by John of Salisbury who died in 1180. It deals with various occupations held by the Church to be harmful, and refers to the fate of those who practise them. The name of the ambassador sent to Corinth is there given as Chilon.

604 'In ful greet honour', thus showing respect to the people of Corinth; his attitude changed when he found them dicing.

605 **to maken hire alliaunce** To make alliance with them.

Lacedaemon is Sparta

608 **hem** Objective case to 'fond' and in apposition to 'alle . . . lond' in line 607.

610 **stal hym** Stole away. The word '**stal**' suggests some kind of secrecy.

611 **ther** i.e. in Corinth.

name Reputation.

612 **defame** Disgrace.

613 **yow** The people of Lacedaemon.

615 'To me it would be preferable to die', 'I would rather die'.

619 **As by my tretee** By any treaty of mine.

620 **hee** Is usually written 'he'. Here it is emphatic, as a rhyme with tretee.

621 The King of Parthia sent the dice to Demetrius.

the book See note on line 603.

623 '**him**' Is repeated as is 'hem' in 608.

peire Set. In the *General Prologue* the Prioress's rosary is called a 'peire of bedes'.

624 **used hasard** Given way to dicing.

ther-biforn On some previous occasion. It is not clear who this King Demetrius was.

627 **lordes** Men of noble birth.

may can.

oother maner pley Some other kind of amusement.

628 **honeste** Honourable, reputable.

to dryve the day awey To make the time pass quickly.

629 Having delivered homilies against gluttony and dicing, the

Pardoner turns to the use of oaths. To swear at all is monstrous, he says: to swear that a thing is true when it is false is more monstrous still. The reference to St Matthew is to the verse where he says 'swear not at all'. Matthew, 5,34.

630 **trete** Requires an object 'As old books treat the subject'.

632 **reprevable** Blameworthy. The word 'reprevable' seems weak after 'abhominable'.

633 **heighe** This is the weak form of the adjective **heigh**, following the article *the*.

634 **witnesse on Mathew** This queer phrase means ' as St Matthew testifies', or 'call St Matthew as witness'.

635 The quotation from the Prophet Jeremiah is indicated in several MSS of *The Canterbury Tales*, and found in Chapter 4, Verse 2. Chaucer misquotes it, however, or puts an inaccurate quotation in the Pardoner's mouth.

636 **sooth** Truly.

637 **doom** Judgement.

638 **ydel sweryng** Pointless swearing.

cursednesse Wickedness.

639 **the firste table** These Commandments tell us of our duty to God. The Second Table instructs us in our duty to our neighbours. 'Thou shalt not take the name of the Lord thy God in vain' is the Third Commandment according to the arrangement of the Authorized Version, but the Second, according to the Vulgate, which, of course, Chaucer used.

643 **rather** Earlier. Chaucer's argument seems to be that the Commandments are arranged in order of importance, and therefore the Second Commandment is more important in God's sight than those which follow.

646 **knowen** They know.

648 **forther over** Moreover.

al plat Plainly.

649 The quotation is from Ecclesiasticus, 23,11

vengeance scourge.

from his hous From the house of him.

650 **to outrageous** Too violent.

651–5 Here are examples of violent oaths.

651 **nayles** Here the reference is clearly to the nails of Christ's body. See line 288, and note.

652 **The blood ... that is in Hayles** The Abbey of Hailes, near Winchcombe, Gloucestershire, claimed to have in a phial a portion of

the Blood of Christ – a most precious relic, which became visible to a penitent who had obtained forgiveness.

653–5 The player swears by the arms of God. The game is the game of Hasard, still played under the name of Craps. The rules are explained in the standard work, *Hoyle's Games*. The caster has thrown his two dice and scored seven: his opponent has thrown a five and a three, or eight. Each has one more cast, it seems, and the caster curses the other in advance should he fail to make a bigger total than the first does.

656 **this fruyt cometh of** This is the result of . . . The result is set out in line 657. '**The bicched bones two**' refers to the two dice used in the game. The work '**bicched**', means 'accursed'.

659 **lete** Set aside, forsake.

660 He turns to his tale again, which he had left after line 482.

661 **riotoures** Revellers, rather than rioters. He has not yet mentioned them. They are to be the chief characters of the Tale.

662 **Erst er** Before.

Prime The first service of the day – taking place during the hour after sunrise.

Bell Possibly that of a striking clock, or of a summons to worship.

663 **were set hem** Had sat themselves down.

664 **clynke** Tinkle; not the same deep sound as '**rong**' of line 662. The sexton headed the procession to the graveyard, and thus summoned prayers for the dead person.

665 **his** Its. There was no possessive of the word 'it' till the end of the sixteenth century. 'Its' is first recorded in print in 1598. 'His' was written till then, though 'its' may have been spoken.

666 **that oon** That suggests the leader, the most notable of the group. It is used like Latin '*ille*'.

knave Servant, like German 'knabe'.

667 **gan callen** Gan is an auxiliary verb, making a past tense.

'**Gan to callen**' would mean 'began to call'.

go bet Go along, though 'bet' is really a comparative adverb; '**redily**' also means 'quickly'.

668 **heer forby** Past here.

669 **weel** Carefully.

670 **it nedeth** There is no need for that; '**nedeth**' is an impersonal verb.

672 **felawe** Companion.

673 **to-nyght** This very night. We should say 'Last night', though the context suggests that the time of the conversation was very early in the morning. They had begun their revelry long before the first service in the church, and the boy had heard the news two hours previously.

674 for-dronke Very drunk. '**For-**' is an intensive prefix.

upright The usual meaning of the word is 'with face upwards', but we are told he was sitting on his bench. The word here seems to have its modern meaning of 'straight up'.

675 privee theef A secret thief, to steal away his life.

men clepeth People call. The relative pronoun object of 'clepeth' is omitted.

679 The line suggests that the cause of death was the plague, which was carried by the black rat.

680 his presence The presence of Death.

681 me thynketh It seems to me. Do not translate by 'I think'. The verb is impersonal.

682 be war of Be on your guard against.

683 beth Be.

evermoore At all times.

684 my dame My mother.

687 'Within a village, over a mile from here'.

688 The 'false traytour' had attacked all sorts and conditions of men.

hyne A peasant.

page An attendant in a castle.

689 'I should think he has his dwelling there.'

690 'It would be very wise to be on your guard.'

dishonour Harm.

692 Goddes armes Another 'outrageous othe'.

693–4 His drinking had given him courage, and boastfulness.

wey and strete Path and paved road.

695 digne Holy.

696 we thre been al ones We three are all of one mind.

697 A form of oath-taking. They would be sworn brothers to one another.

700 Another suggestion of the man's bravado.

705 al dronken Quite drunk.

rage Excitement.

708 Their 'grisly oothes' have been mentioned in line 473.

709 A further reference to their 'othes': see line 474.

712 wolde han troden Were about to cross.

713 There was only **one** man. He was old and poor. Contrast the meekness of the old man with the boisterousness of the three young ones.

715 **Lordes** A complimentary form of address.

God yow see May God look on you with His favour.

716 **proudeste** Most arrogant. He was doubtless the leader of the group, and had spoken the words in lines 692–701.

717 **answerde agayn** Replied rudely, to the old man's blessing.

'what!' is an exclamation' 'how now!'

carl Fellow.

with sory grace Confound you.

718 **artow** Art thou. **Thou** would be used contemptuously.

for-wrapped Intensive; wrapped up *closely*.

719 **lyvestow** Do you live on.

720 **gan looke** Looked. See line 667 note.

722 'Though I should walk as far as India' – an almost unimaginable distance.

724 **wolde** Would be willing to.

725 **stille** Permanently, continuously.

727 'Nor alas will death take my life away.' At the reference to Death, whom the three were seeking, no doubt they pricked up their ears, but they let the old man continue what he had to say.

728 **walke** Walk about, suggesting the monotony of his existence, as does also the word '**kaityf**', meaning captive, or prisoner, deprived of freedom.

729 **my moodres gate** My mother's gate, his mother being the earth.

730 **knokke with my staf** Tap the ground as I walk along.

732 **vanysshe** Fade away.

734–6 The **cheste** is the long treasure chest into which a man would put his valuables, such as clothes, and articles he valued for the sake of association. As a rule it would be placed at the foot of his bed. He would give up all his treasures in exchange for a hair winding-sheet, to be wrapped round his dead body at once.

737 **grace** Favour.

738 'And therefore is my face all pale and withered.'

739 **sires** The politeness of the old man is in great contrast to the surliness of the others. 'It is no courtesy on your part to speak insults to an old man'.

743 **agayns** In the presence of.

744 'You ought to stand up.'

748 **wher ye go or ryde** 'Go' means 'walk'. The phrase is a conventional way of saying 'whatever happens'. If you ride you are rich: if you walk you are poor.

wher Whether.

749 **as I have to go** See line 733, and 728. He cannot rest.

751 **this oother hasardour** the words do not imply that a second gambler is now speaking.

752 'You do not part from us so easily as this.'

755 **have heer my trouthe** You take my word for it.

756 **thou shalt it abye** You shall pay for it.

758 **of his assent** In his conspiracy.

764 The double negative produces a stronger negative. 'Not in any way because of your boasting will he hide himself at all.'

765 **right there** See note on line 753.

766 'May God who redeemed mankind save you and restore you.'

770–71 'Nearly eight bushels of weight, as it seemed to them, of fine round florins, coined in gold.' The nominal value of a florin was six shillings.

778 **wit** Intelligence, wisdom.

bourde Jest, play the fool.

780 **to lyven** So that we may live.

782 **wende** Would have thought.

784 **myghte** If the gold might.

789 **stronge** Violent; treasure trove, even in Chaucer's day, belonged to the King.

790 **doon us honge** Have us hanged.

792 'As skilfully and secretly as possible.'

793 **Cut** Lots. The shortest straw drawn from a number held in the hand indicated the man on whom the lot fell.

798 **subtilly** Carefully, cunningly.

803 **it** The shortest straw.

808 **my sworne brother** See line 698.

809 'Something to your profit.'

812 **departed** Shared.

813 **shape** Arrange.

815 **hadde I nat doon** Should I not have done.

817 **he** The other one.

822 **graunte** Promise.

823 **biwreye** Expose.

826 **looke** Notice.

827 **pleye** Jest, sport.

833 **lustes** Desires, whether good or bad.

838 **rolleth up and doun** Ponders in his mind.

840 **if so were that I myghte** If only I might.

843 **murye** Happily.

847 **for-why** Because.

in swich lyvyng In such a state of mind.

848 **leve** Permission. Even the devil recognized his baseness, and thought him better out of the way, for the reason suggested in lines 849, 850.

852 **pothecarie** Apothecary, seller of drugs and poisons.

855 **polcat** A sort of weasel.

856 **capouns** Fowls.

857 **wreke hym** Avenge himself.

858 **vermyn** Stealthy, slinking animals.

destroy Annoy, cause destruction.

hym An 'ethic' dative: he was the person affected by the destruction.

860 **al so** As, introducing a wish.

862 **confiture** Preparation.

863 **noght but the montance** No more than the amount.

865 **sterve** Die (not starve).

866 'At walking pace no more than a mile.'

871 **hym** For himself.

874 'Was getting himself ready to toil.'

876 **with sory grace** Here the phrase seems to mean 'the wretched fellow'.

879 **sermone** Make a long speech about it.

880 **cast** Arranged, planned.

882 **that oon** Presumably the first speaker, who had suggested the murder.

889 **Avycen** Avicenna who lived in the eleventh century was one of the great authorities on medicine in the Middle Ages. The doctor whose learning Chaucer indicates in the *General Prologue* had studied him. He was a Persian, whose famous treatise on medicine was translated into Latin under the title of **Canon Medicinae**. By '**canon**' here, Chaucer means rules for compounding prescriptions. The word '**fen**' is the Arabic for section. Nothing Avicenna wrote described more remarkable symptoms of the effect of poisons than the effects of the poison on the two victims.

894 The story of the three revellers ends with this line. A few exclamatory remarks follow.

895 **of** Above.

896 **traytours** Treacherous.

homycide Murder.

897 **glotonye, luxurie, hasardrye** Were three of the crimes the Pardoner set out to pillory.

898 **vileyne** Wickedness.

899 **usage and pride** Habit and arrogance.

900 **bitide** Come about.

901 **which that** Who.

903 **unkynde** Unnatural, ungrateful.

905 **ware yow** Do you beware.

906 **warice** Heal, guard.

907 **nobles** Were worth six shillings and eight pence then;
sterlynges Were silver pennies.

910 **wyves** Women, whether married or single.

wolle Wool.

914 **clene** Pure.

cleer Spotless.

916 **leche** Healer, curer, doctor.

919 **tale** Story.

920 **pardoun** Indulgences.

925 **kneleth heere adoun** Kneel down here, on this road to Canterbury.

926 **mekely** Humbly.

929 He is never tired of reminding his potential converts of the necessity of contributing to his collection.

931 They are lucky to have a pardoner with them as a sort of insurance against misfortune on the highway. He would be ready to administer the last rites if necessary, and a soul would be comforted.

945 He offers to accept no more than a groat from the Host, although he is the deepest sinner of them all.

946–55 The violence and obscenity of the Host's response caused these lines to be expunged from editions of Chaucer for many years. They can be regarded as the Pardoner's 'reward' for the shameless immorality of his life and the hypocrisy of his preaching, on the part of the company he is addressing.

947 **theech** This is contracted from 'thee ich', I prosper. The words mean 'I can assure you'.

952 Saint Helena was believed to have discovered the cross on which Christ was crucified.

960 The knight interferes in what promises to become a quarrel. He makes the two kiss one another and be friends.

966 **neer** Nearer. The word is comparative.

Chaucer's narrative art in the *Tale*
The characters

Far and away the most significant figure in the poem is the Pardoner himself. Almost everything in it bears his stamp. Before considering the teller of the tale, however, we should look at the characters within his narrative. Those to be considered are the three revellers, the old man whom they meet in their search, the inn-keeper and the boy in the tavern. (We can leave aside the apothecary who sells the poison at the end of the story.)

The trio of *'rioters'* are scarcely distinguished one from another. One appears to be the dominant partner, proposing that they should form an alliance to 'sleen this false traytour Deeth', and it is presumably this one, 'the proudeste' and 'the worste of hem', who speaks so abusively to the old man and later puts forward the idea to his companion that they should betray the third and kill him. But the three villains are not really given distinct, separate identities – they do not even have the dignity of being named. Rather it is their similarity to one another that is stressed. They have the same vices; together they go in search of death, together they find the pile of gold that halts their search; the notion of murder occurs to two of them simultaneously (the other is a little slow-witted, although ready enough to assent to the slaying of the third when the plot is explained). None is less guilty than the others. This lack of individuality is intended by the author. The story is too compressed to allow for description or development of character. Within the narrative itself there is no decorative or spare material: everything contributes to the hasty unfolding of events. Elaborate characterization would be a luxury – we already know all we need to know about the three bad men – as well as a brake on the story's accelerating progress. In addition, if we knew more about the men we might begin to sympathize with them or, at least, to regard them as individual human beings rather than as mere embodiments of vice and folly whose fate is thoroughly deserved.

The *boy* and the *inn-keeper* have very minor roles. The *boy* provides a vivid picture (lines 670–684) of the abrupt death of the revellers' acquaintance, and concludes his account with some proverbial wisdom passed on to him by his mother, 'Beth redy for to meete hym (i.e. Death) evermoore.' The tavern-keeper confirms the boy's story and refers to a nearby village where everybody has died within a year as a result of the plague. In the child's and the adult's attitude – fearful and respectful towards death – we can see a contrast to the headstrong approach of the three revellers who rush off in the direction of the dead village, quite oblivious to the advice of the others on the need for caution and preparation in the face of death.

The *old man* whom they encounter on the way is the most puzzling figure in the Tale. Although nameless, he is the only character to be provided with any sort of external description, even if nothing about him appears very remarkable: he is 'al forwrapped' except for his face, which is 'ful pale and welked'; he is old and poor and walks with a staff. It is partly the lack of detail which has provoked much speculation about this figure and his significance in the story. At one extreme he has been taken to be no more than his realistic description might suggest, an old man who is frightened by three threatening young ones and who therefore gives them a direction to 'death' (which happens to lead by accident to the hoard of gold) so as to get rid of them and give himself time to get away. At the other extreme the old man has been interpreted symbolically, even taken as the figure of Death itself.

There is no necessity to arrive at a precise answer as to who the old man is or what he represents, even if such an answer were possible. Here suggestion may be more effective than explicit statement. There are elements of realism in the old man's presentation – a touch of self-pity when he refers to his great age, a modest dignity when he replies to the aggression of his questioners – but there are also some aspects of his appearance and words which hint at something beyond the ordinary. Like the three revellers he is searching for death, not to destroy it, as they intend, but to put an end to his own exhausted life: in anguish he asks, 'whan shul my bones been at reste?' Paradoxically, although he cannot obtain death for himself, he is able to procure it for others – he tells the trio, 'in that grove I lafte hym (death) by my fay'. At one moment he laments his failure to find death, at the next he is giving instructions on where it is to be found. One explanation for this contradiction has already been mentioned, that he gives them death's whereabouts as a means of getting rid of them and in ignorance of what they will find under the oak tree. A rather more plausible explanation still keeps us within the bounds of 'realism'. The old man knows that there is a pile of gold coins in the grove of trees, he knows the kind of men he is dealing with, he can probably foresee the murderous dissension that will spring up when the three have found the treasure. The money does not represent death for him. He is distressed not by poverty but by unending age. On the other hand, the money does bring death for the revellers – in accordance with the old man's direction – because of the kind of people they are.

This 'realistic' appraisal of the old man's words and actions, however, comes afterwards and with hindsight. On a first reading of this part of the poem we are likely to notice other things: the sinister and baffling irony that, while searching unsuccessfully for death himself, he is nevertheless able to point others along the 'croked wey' to extinction; the contrast between his age and the rioters' youth, his courtesy and their roughness. The most important difference between them is perhaps that, although desperate for death, he is at the same time resigned to live for 'as longe tyme as it is Goddes wille' and will not deliberately shorten his life; the young men however are eaten up with a frantic impatience. Looked at in a certain light, even the fairly conventional description of the old man's appearance can take on a strange cast. The garments that enclose him completely except for his withered face recall a shroud wrapped round a corpse. The innocent-seeming stick, a natural prop of old age, becomes the instrument with which he knocks 'on the ground, which is my moodres gate' asking for re-admittance (i.e. burial) – a bizarre conception of a familiar object. The sparsity of detail, the 'corpse-like' appearance, his knowledge of death's whereabouts, all combine to make this nameless character a figure of suggestive ambiguity. We do not have to decide exactly who or what he is, but we are able to appreciate the placing of this puzzling man at the mid-point of the story where his own quest crosses, at a stile, the opposing search of the revellers.

The Pardoner

The principal character of the poem is the Pardoner himself. It is necessary to understand something of the Pardoner's job, in general terms, before considering Chaucer's particular creation. A pardoner was licensed to preach in churches and to appeal for money to support some definite object. Perhaps funds had to be raised to finance a crusade or to construct a church. Those who made a contribution had their reward in the shape of the remission of some part of a penance for a sin which they had confessed and which had been forgiven by the priest. In fact, Chaucer's Pardoner claims to be able to absolve – cleanse or free – people not merely from doing penance for their sins but from the sins themselves. In other words, he is taking on the role of a priest. Such a system of 'buying' forgiveness was obviously open to abuse, and it is evident that corruption was widespread among pardoners. By fraudulent practices they obtained money which was never accounted for. The situation became scandalous, and pardoners were finally suppressed by the Council of Trent in 1562.

Chaucer's Pardoner sets something of a standard for shamelessness and corruption. The description of him in *The Prologue to The Canterbury Tales* is that of a confidence trickster. He uses fake relics – a pillow-case which he claims 'was Oure Lady veyl', a glass container of pig's bones passed off as the remains of a saint – to impress, and to make easier his lifelong task, parting simple people from their money. We learn that he makes more money in a single day than a poor parson earns in two months. He is expert at preaching, for he depends upon his oratorical skills to gain a good living. His appearance and his manner leave the Canterbury pilgrims in no doubt as to the sort of person he is. They protest that they have no wish to hear a crude story (line 324) when the Host offers the Pardoner a chance to tell a tale. He agrees that he will tell his fellow-travellers 'som honeste thyng' but first demands a breathing-space – or rather a drinking space – in a tavern which the company happens to be passing.

The 'draughte of moyste and corny ale' which the Pardoner drinks before embarking on his story has often been held responsible for the recklessness with which he exposes the tricks of his trade to the other pilgrims. Only the effect of drink, it is said, could explain the open-ness of his revelation of hypocrisy and deceit. And certainly, in what follows, the Pardoner damns himself completely. He prides himself on his imposing delivery of a sermon:

'I peyne me to han an hauteyn speche,
And rynge it out as round as gooth a belle'

and on reinforcing his words with movements (395–8). His
sermons are dramatic performances, entertaining as well as
instructive for his congregation. This preacher has no intention
of imitating Christ's disciples; instead he takes pleasure in his
ruthless denial of Christian principle:

'I wol noon of the Apostles countrefete:
I wol have moneie, wolle, chese, and whete,
Al were it yeven of the povereste page,
Or of the povereste wydwe in a village,
Al sholde hir children sterve for famyne.'

He relishes the ironic contradiction that makes greed both the
object of this condemnation as well as his only motive in
preaching – 'Thus kan I preche agayn that same vice/Which that
I use.' A side benefit of delivering a sermon is that it offers the
opportunity for settling old scores against anyone who has dared
to criticize the Pardoner or his colleagues (412–22). Sermons
may be used for any purpose, in fact – as long as it is a perver-
sion of the aim of preaching.

The Pardoner's self-condemnation is absolute. He is, as he
says with satisfaction, 'a ful vicious man'. Such revelations are
not so inherently improbable as they might seem. As suggested
above, the Pardoner's tongue may be unfastened by drink. The
audience he is addressing, the comparatively sophisticated mixture of Canterbury pilgrims, is some way removed from the
simple country congregations he usually faces. In front of his
present audience – including educated figures like the knight,
the doctor, the scholar – he wants to show not merely an
example of his sermon but to reveal the cunning mechanism
underlying it. Perhaps he is elated by the prospect of being
exactly what he is, that 'ful vicious man', rather than hiding
behind a pious exterior, as he must hide for most of his life. We
should remember too that such villainous 'frankness' is in itself a
literary convention and a means of characterization, one found
outside Chaucer (e.g. in Shakespeare's *Richard III*).

Other problems and questions concerning the Pardoner
remain. There is the incongruity of such a corrupt individual
telling such a 'moral tale', although here the story-teller has
anticipated us and makes a point of referring to this contradiction (459–61) – he has the best of reasons, in his own eyes, for

upholding morality: it has earned him a 'hundred marks' since he took up this lucrative business. In any case it could be argued that the tone of the *Tale* is very much a reflection of its teller and that the contradiction between the two is more apparent than real (see *Themes* for a fuller discussion of this topic).

Greater difficulty arises when we consider the story-teller's behaviour at the conclusion of his narrative. After giving a terse description of the deaths of the three revellers the Pardoner launches into a strident condemnation of the sins connected with their downfall ('O glotonye, luxurie, and hasardrye!' etc). This moderates into a lament for man's ingratitude to Christ (900–903) and then descends to a sales' pitch as the speaker describes the forgiveness he can offer if the price is right ('So that ye offre nobles, or sterlynges...'). This is his 'act' as he performs it in front of a congregation, an act that appears to conclude in the words, to the Canterbury pilgrims, 'and lo, sires, thus I preche!' The demonstration is over and we might expect the 'sincerity' of the sermonizing to be replaced by the mocking tone employed by the Pardoner in the Prologue to his story. In fact, he continues rather unexpectedly:

'And Jhesu Crist, that is oure soules leche,
So graunte you his pardoun to receyve,
For that is best, I wol yow nat deceyve!'

This passage has sometimes been interpreted as an unprecedented outburst of sincerity on the part of the Pardoner. In proclaiming that he will not deceive his hearers (now apparently the Canterbury pilgrims rather than the simple country congregation he has been addressing in his imagination) he turns his back for a moment on a self-satisfied existence of hypocrisy and falsehood. Is this a genuine moment of remorse or is the announcement that he will not deceive his fellow-pilgrims a further example of deception, more proof of the Pardoner's skill in conveying intense sincerity through his words?

We cannot know for certain whether Chaucer's Pardoner is here expressing genuine piety or just being supremely artful. It is worth bearing in mind, however, that such an appeal for grace rounds off a number of *The Canterbuty Tales* and is therefore not unique to the Pardoner. Genuine or not, the appeal is soon followed by a more characteristic and jokey insolence. He explains to his companions how fortunate they are to 'have a suffisant Pardoneer' on the pilgrimage. If any sinner will offer money and kneel down he will receive pardon, or, for the traveller's greater convenience and comfort, pardons can actually be given on the way, 'al newe and fressh at every miles ende'. It is hardly possible to believe that the Pardoner is being anything other than mischievously impudent here. He cannot have forgotten the extent of his earlier self-exposure to the pilgrims, and he cannot now expect to be taken seriously. That he is spurred on by mischief, rather than by a realistic belief that he can make money, is shown by the nonchalant way in which he refers to the hazards of travel:

'Paraventure ther may fallen oon or two
Doun of his hors, and breke his nekke atwo'

– in the event of an accident he is there as a kind of spiritual break-down service. The humour – albeit slightly unfeeling – of such remarks is very evidently at odds with the intense (and false) 'sincerity' of his earlier preaching. In addition, he ends his speech with the suggestion that the Host should be the first to offer money for forgiveness 'for he is moost envoluped in synne'. The Host chooses to see the insult rather than the humour of the remark, and his violent and imaginative obscenities in reply to the Pardoner serve to reduce even that 'ful vicious man', usually so eloquent in both his deceit and his self-revelation, to an angry silence. The man who lives by his tongue has been lashed by another's.

Structure and narrative

The Pardoner is invited by the Host to tell a story. The poem
which follows is divided into Prologue and Tale. The Prologue is
a mixture of direct statement to the pilgrims, where the Pardoner unreservedly exposes his preaching technique and tricks,
and repetition of the very words he uses before a simple and
credulous congregation. We learn of the way he softens up his
church audience by his exhibition of (fake) relics and his attrib-
ution of near-magical powers to such bits of bone and cloth. The
'frame' which the Prologue provides for the Tale not only offers
us a sharp self-portrait of a 'con' man but is essential for a full
appreciation of the Tale that follows. Without the benefit of the
Pardoner's self-revelation in the Prologue we might be tempted
to take the sermon as no more than a vigorous and sombre
example of medieval preaching, delivered with unusual drive
and skill but essentially straightforward. Our knowledge of the
Pardoner's real self, however, throws our responses out: we note
the nature of the Tale but, above all, we note the nature of the
teller. The poem is richer and more complex for its introduction
and conclusion where the Pardoner speaks with unabashed
directness to the other pilgrims – and to us – rather than mas-
querading as a hell-fire preacher.

The substance of his Tale is the sermon he has thundered out
from the pulpit many times before. It is made up of two sections,
the narrative of the three revellers and the extended denunciation of various sins which precedes it. The forbidding story is a
typical medieval 'exemplum' (example) inserted in the sermon
to illustrate those sins in dramatic action. The Pardoner has a
good reason for telling 'olde stories':

'For lewed peple loven tales olde,
Swiche thynges kan they wel reporte and holde.'

Shrewdly, he begins speaking from the pulpit with the story. He
mentions the setting (Flanders) and the 'compaignye' of revellers. Having alerted his audience with this 'once upon a time'
opening (signified by the word 'whilom'), instead of fulfilling
expectations by a continuation of the narrative he launches into

an enthusiastic catalogue of mankind's sinfulness. Perhaps the promise of a story to come would in itself hold the congregation's attention, but the preacher takes care to offer a variety of subject-matter, tone and pitch in his guide to sinning. He not only has to interest his hearers, he must establish his authority over them as a preacher. The Pardoner has a long list of examples, drawn from the Bible and classical sources, which illustrate the perils of sin and also serve to establish his intellectual credentials. He can play at being the scholar and teacher –

'. . . avyseth yow right wel
What was comaunded unto Lamuel, –
Nat Samuel, but Lamuel seye I;
Redeth the Bible, and fynde it expresly
Of wyn-yevyng to hem that han justice.'

This sort of thing is said merely as a means of asserting his mental superiority over his listeners; few of them would be really concerned over the problem of 'the giving of wine to people who dispense justice', and fewer still would have been able to read the Bible – or anything else – to check his pedantic references.

At other moments the Pardoner can be a realistic observer of the world around him; of the drunk man, he says,

'Sour is thy breeth, foul artow to embrace,
And thurgh thy dronke nose semeth the soun,
As though thou seydest ay, 'Sampsoun, Sampsoun!'

and even this piece of mimicry can be neatly turned to make a little lesson in the next line,

'And yet, God woot, Sampsoun drank nevere no wyn.'

The Pardoner is coarsely direct at some points –

'. . . and fouler is the dede
Whan man so drynketh of the white and rede,
That of his throte he maketh his pryvee,
Thurgh thilke cursed superfluitee.'

– but he is equally capable of acting the high-minded moralizer:

'Gret sweryng is a thyng abhominable,
And fals sweryng is yet moore reprevable.'

Such a varied approach to his task of denunciation ensures his hearers' attention.

The tale itself (661–894) unrolls with extraordinary rapidity. As already explained in the section *The Characters*, no unnecessary detail is allowed to intrude – the bare essentials of character are revealed in dialogue, the story is furnished with a few vital 'props' (the pile of gold, the three bottles for the poisoned wine) like an unadorned medieval drama.

Our sense of pace is reinforced by the fact that the events depicted in the narrative take place within a single day. At the beginning the revellers are drinking in the tavern 'longe erst er prime rong of any belle' (i.e., very early in the morning) and they die at each other's hands before nightfall, the time when they had planned to carry off the treasure in secret. The 'pilgrimage' of life towards death, which for the old man has already lasted too many weary years, is compressed for the young men into a single fevered day. They start out drunk and then, on discovering the gold, become so intoxicated with greed that they resort to murder. They approach their destruction in ignorance and also with eagerness; their haste is literal and contributes to the tale's rapid tempo:

'And up they stirte, al dronken, in this rage . . .'
'And everich of thise riotoures ran
Til he cam to that tree . . .'
'And forth he gooth, no lenger wolde he tarie,
Into the toun . . .'
'This cursed man hath in his hond y-hent
This poysoun in a box, and sith he ran
Into the nexte strete . . .'

The revellers never rest content for a second. If they are not running somewhere, they are scheming or boasting – that they will kill Death, that they will spend their lives in gambling – and these delusions have something of the same hectic quality as their physical movements. This reckless abandon of the sinners as they race for death is emphasized by a narrative that never pauses for an ornamental description or a moralistic aside. There is no time to look at the view in *The Pardoner's Tale*.

The narrative travels most quickly at its close. Little more than twenty lines (868–88) are needed to describe the purchase of the poison, the bottles of wine to put in it, the return of the youngest reveller, his death and the deaths of his two 'partners'. As the Pardoner says, 'What nedeth it to sermone of it moore?' The second part of the story, in particular, operates with the smooth-

appropriate to this bare narrative that in the end any attractive human element is banished and the plotting and counter-plotting of the tale's conclusion acquire a mechanical inevitability which satisfies our sense of poetic justice and our need for narrative organization.

Themes

At one level the themes of *The Pardoner's Tale* are so apparent as to require little comment. The poem is, in large part, a version of the sermon which the Pardoner has so frequently delivered to enrich himself. In the course of his oration the preacher attacks several sins – gluttony, swearing, the evils attendant on gambling – and takes as his principal subject or theme the Latin saying: *Radix malorum est Cupiditas* ('Cupidity is the root of all evil'). Naturally enough, the story proves the correctness of the moral statement and love of money is shown to be the cause of the young men's downfall and deaths. The corruption of the preacher himself, amply revealed in his Prologue, is further testimony to the truth of the old saying: the Pardoner's hypocrisy, callousness, contempt, all his vices, may be said to spring from one source, his own avarice.

We might say, therefore, that the themes of *The Pardoner's Tale* are those that could have been the subjects of many medieval sermons: the wastefulness of sin, the dangers of vice, the need for grace, etc. Yet it is probably fair to say too that most readers' understanding of what the poem is primarily about is not adequately reflected in a few straightforward moral tags. One reason for this is, of course, that the Pardoner ruthlessly undermines the creed he himself proclaims. He takes pleasure in stressing in front of the company of pilgrims:

'For myn entente is nat but for to wynne,
And no thyng for correccioun of synne . . .'

The fact that the pardoner does not believe his own words – or at the least, that he does not take them to heart – immediately adds a disconcerting element to our responses. There appears to be an irresolvable contradiction between the rigorous morality of the story and the debased nature of its teller, and this indicates that we cannot at once accept the preacher's own explanation of his subject matter.

If we wish to grasp *The Pardoner's Tale*, therefore, we must look beyond the Pardoner's ostensible themes and topics and examine his language and his preoccupations. Within this character there is obviously a split – more, perhaps, an abyss – between a virtuous 'public' preacher and a profoundly corrupt 'private' self. This split becomes evident both in what the Pardoner says and the way in which he says it.

The Tale can be interpreted as a fitting mirror to its teller. It is sombre and violent, restless and disordered, half in love with what it is condemning. In his Prologue the Pardoner explains how he uses the pulpit as the place to 'spitte out my venym under hewe/Of hoolynesse'. The same 'poison under cover of holiness' infects the tale. It begins with a tremendous denunciation of the various vices in which the revellers indulge, but there is entertainment and pleasure in the denunciation, for both speaker and listeners. The force with which the Pardoner launches his attacks on sins and sinners indicates the latent violence in his temperament. As the revellers tear Christ's body verbally by their oaths, so too does the Pardoner wrench parts of the body away from the whole:

'O wombe! O bely! O stynking cod!'
'Allas! the shorte throte, the tendre mouth . . .'

In this enumeration of sins, their branches and their consequences, there is the enthusiasm of the devotee. He *knows* what he is talking about. Something of his pleasure in the business of condemnation is also suggested by the way in which he transfers his sights from one human failing to another –

'And now I have yspoke of glotonye,
Now wol I yow deffenden hasardrye'

– as if the process of denunciation has acquired a momentum which is more important than the sins themselves. For all his methodical approach, the Pardoner makes little attempt to discriminate between sins; indeed, committing one seems to entail having to commit all the others:

'Hasard is verray mooder of lesynges,
And of deceite, and cursed forswerynges.
Blaspheme of Crist, manslaughtre, and wast also
Of catel, and of tyme . . .'

although here the least serious of the consequences of gambling ('waste of goods and time') is placed last, after blasphemy and manslaughter, probably in deliberate anti-climax. As the sermon unfolds, so one vice leads inexorably to another: drunken-ness stimulates lust and is itself a kind of gluttony; gambling leads to lies, anger, etc.

Almost all these vices, and not avarice alone, are embodied in the three revellers. The introduction to the narrative presents a picture of mankind as a whole inescapably bound by the ball and chain of its sinfulness. There are a couple of references to Christ's redemption in the course of the Pardoner's preaching, but they have a perfunctory air. Naturally, the preacher dwells on the badness of his fellow-men − there is small profit to be made from their goodness − but we sense his glee in the task of condemnation. He would sooner denounce than praise.

This double vision, by which the Pardoner is enabled both to condemn and enjoy, is well shown by his attack on gluttony. Vigorous disgust is registered by the line beginning 'O wombe . . .' (already quoted) but something more ambiguous is shown by his knowledgeable concern with how food is made fit for the glutton-gourmet:

'Out of the harde bones knokke they
The mary, for they caste noght awey
That may go thurgh the golet softe and swoote.
Of spicerie, of leef, and bark, and roote,
Shal been his sauce y-maked by delit,
To make hym yet a newer appetit . . .'

This fine re-creation of the cooks' skills betrays the Pardoner's real interests. Similarly, he preaches against 'blasphemous oaths' but gives enough examples at this point (651–55) and later in the story for us to suspect that he rather enjoys the violence of such expressions as well as the opportunity to utter them 'under cover' of a sermon.

If the introductory material paints a bleak and misanthropic picture of man's vice and weakness, then the story of the revellers gives to that picture a dramatic force and particularity. The Tale shows, with stony literalism, that the wages of sin is death. Death itself is not merely the object of the trio's quest but the dominant feature of the story. It opens with a bell clinking before a corpse on the way to the grave and the boy's account of how the man came to die. There are references to the plague, which has killed all the inhabitants of a nearby village. The life of the old man is devoted to a search for death. No sooner have the revellers discovered the hoard of gold than they are plotting to kill one another. Even the apothecary (chemist) from whom the youngest obtains his poison appears preoccupied with the subject of death as he explains how powerful and rapid is his mixture in its fatal operation. There is barely a piece of dialogue in the poem which is not concerned, directly, with death – and with death envisaged as something violent and sudden ('And with his spere he smoot his herte atwo'; 'I shal ryve hym thurgh the sydes tweye'; 'This poysoun is so strong and violent'). Death, obviously, cannot be escaped, but in this poem the fact of it is thrust in the foreground and casts its shadow over the entire work.

In Chaucer's lifetime the Black Death had devastated Europe. The first, and worst, outbreak affected England in 1348/9. At a rough estimate something like one in three of the population died as a result of the plague. It was not unknown for whole communities to wither away, as the inn-keeper says. A common, and understandable, response to this catastrophe was to explain the outbreak as God's means of punishing man's sinfulness, perhaps because any explanation was better than none. It is not surprising that we find in this poem – the most darkly shaded of *The Canterbury Tales* – an overwhelming concern with sin and death, together with a strident insistence on the connection between the two. It is the genius of Chaucer's art that provides a frame for these obsessions and puts them in the context of the Pardoner's revelations about himself. The result is that, rather than being an energetic example of medieval preaching or 'only' a fine story, the poem as a whole becomes a kind of monument to a figure who radiates something of the same fascinating and disturbing quality as the tale he tells.

Irony and humour

Irony is to be found everywhere in *The Pardoner's Tale*, but the dominant irony is external to the Tale itself – that it is told by a man whose life denies all the principles he so ardently preaches. In particular, the Pardoner is delighted by his sermonizing against his own favourite vice, avarice. The condemnation that he directs at others should be more properly directed against himself (he is a worse man than any member of his congregation). An over-riding irony is that, while the Pardoner appears to have the last laugh at the expense of his simple hearers, we are encouraged to apply the lesson of his sermon to himself, for he is as greedy and unscrupulous as the three 'revellers' and as deserving of 'punishment' as they are. The last laugh may be on him, and certainly it is in the poem, as Chaucer describes how 'al the peple lough' after hearing the Host's inventive abuse of the Pardoner.

Within the narrative there are multiple ironies. For example, the parallel quests of the three young men and the old one are ironically dissimilar in their outcomes. The trio dies, while wishing individually to live; the old man lives, despite the strength of his desire for death. An often-noted irony is the moment of the gold's discovery –

'No lenger thanne after Deeth they soughte,
But ech of hem so glad was of that sighte . . .'

At the very point at which they abandon their search they have, in fact, been discovered by death (because their greed for the money leads to their killing each other). Another obvious example of irony is the plotting and counter-plotting by the revellers at the end of the story.

There is little real humour in *The Pardoner's Prologue and Tale* – at least, not of the kind that we are accustomed to recognize as characteristically Chaucerian, in other words a humour that is essentially tolerant and good-natured. Instead we find malice and contempt in the Pardoner's pronouncements: of those he preaches at, he says,

'I rekke nevere whan that they been beryed,
Though that hir soules goon a-blakeberyed.'

Such 'humour' is obviously of a grim and very qualified sort. It is chiefly expressed in the ironic mode and, in this story, we can often term the irony a literal matter of life and death.

Chaucer's verse

The Pardoner's Prologue and Tale is characteristic of Chaucer's mature verse-style in its flexibility and variety. Fittingly, these are also the qualitites required by the Pardoner himself if he is to hold his audience. His style is often declamatory, especially in the lengthy passage on sins (482–660) – many lines begin with an exclamation ('O glotonye, ful of cursednesse!') or a direction ('Looke, Attilla, the grete conqueror . . .'). Equally, the Pardoner's hectic delivery can be modulated to put across the unadorned narrative of the story in all its blunt effectiveness. It is not hard to find examples of the subtlety and refinement of Chaucer's verse and the employment of metre, syntax or sound to reinforce meaning. For instance, in this excerpt dealing with gluttony (that subject close to the Pardoner's heart!):

'Allas! the shorte throte, the tendre mouth,
Maketh that Est and West, and North and South,
In erthe, in eir, in water, men to swynke
To gete a glotoun deyntee mete and drynke.'

The laborious search for delicacies to satisfy the glutton's fastidious appetite is suggested by the repetition of 'and' and the monotonous rhythm of the second and third lines here. The lines are constructed so as to arrive finally, after several intervening phrases, at the object of such a search – 'mete and drynke'. The verse enacts something of the very process of toil and achievement which it describes, meaning is reinforced by the choice of words and their order.

Grammar, pronunciation and versification

Chaucer's language, sometimes called Middle English, represents a transitional stage between Old English (or Anglo-Saxon) and what we speak today. By Chaucer's time English had become a blend of Saxon and the French brought across at the time of the Norman Conquest, but there were distinct dialects in different areas of the country (stronger than modern regional variations). Chaucer's own dialect was the East Midland and, largely because this was the variation of English used in court and government, it was this form of the language that became the standard one. Chaucer's English is recognizably close to us – perhaps closer than might at first sight appear – but there are differences in vocabulary and in the way words work. Such differences are no real barrier to understanding and enjoying Chaucer: the sense of the verse can usually be appreciated without precise grammatical knowledge and it can sometimes be helpful to pronounce aloud an unfamiliar-looking word, the meaning of which may be more apparent in its sound than in its spelling. The latter, incidentally, was not regularized in Chaucer's day, and the same word may be differently spelled in different parts of the text. Middle English was more strongly inflected than its modern counterpart, that is, there was greater variation in the endings of words. For example, where in modern English only the third person singular of the present tense is inflected ('makes', 'falls') in Middle English we find a number of variations to verb-endings in the present tense ('make, makest, maketh, maken).

These very brief notes on grammar may be helpful:
  Noun inflection is very similar to what we are used to in modern English:

-es is almost invariably the mark of the possessive (genitive) case, e.g. 'mannes herte', 'preestes sone', and (e)s indicates the plural, e.g. 'hennes', 'bookes', 'humours'. There are a few exceptions to the standard possessive inflection, e.g. 'fader kin' means 'father's family'.

There are also irregular plurals, mostly familiar ones ('wommen', 'oxen'), a few not ('eyen').

Pronouns: it should be noted that there is no equivalent for 'its' in Middle English. 'His' is used for persons and things, e.g. 'the sonne in his ascencioun'. 'Hir' means both 'her' and 'their', but the context generally makes clear which is intended.

Sometimes the pronoun 'thou' is attached to the verb in a question, e.g. 'woldestow' meaning 'would you'.

The plural of 'that' is 'tho', not 'those'.

Verbs: changes between tenses are not dissimilar to those in modern English. Note that the past participle form of a verb is frequently indicated by the prefix y-, e.g. 'yseyled', 'ywarned'.

Adverbs: in modern English almost all adverbs end '-ly'. This was one of the endings used in Chaucer's day but we also find adverbs ending in '-e' and '-liche'.

Pronunciation

Vowels

Words of English origin

Short vowels

'a' pronounced like 'a' in French placer; but not like 'a' in English 'cat'.

'e' pronounced like 'e' in Modern English 'men'.

'i' pronounced like 'i' in 'pin'. 'y' is often written for 'i', and has the same sound as 'i'.

'o' pronounced like 'o' in 'not'. Before letters written with a number of short strokes, like 'm, n,' and especially a combination of these two, 'o' is written for 'u', but should be pronounced like 'u', as for example, in 'comen, love, somer, monk'.

'u' pronounced like 'u' in 'pull', or like 'oo' in 'soot'; but not like 'u' in 'duke'.

Long vowels

It is often possible to recognize a long vowel by its being duplicated in writing. For example 'taak' contains a long 'a'; 'sooth' contains a long 'o'.

'a' pronounced like 'a' in 'father'.

'e' pronounced like 'e' acute or like 'e' grave in French. Only a knowledge of the origin of the words in Old English can guide the reader to distinguish between the close and open sounds, as they are called, in Chaucer; but the former sound is usually represented in Modern English by 'ee', and the latter by 'ea'. Modern English 'need' had a close vowel in Old English, where it was spelt 'nēd'; Modern English 'mead', a meadow, was 'mēd' in Old English with an open vowel. As an indication that these two vowels had distinct sounds, we may note that Chaucer very rarely makes them rhyme.

'i' (often written 'y'), pronounced like 'ee' in 'feel'.

'o' pronounced either like 'o' in 'so', or like 'a' in 'call'. Chaucer recognizes the different pronunciations just as he distinguishes the two long 'e' sounds. In Modern English the former sound is represented by 'oo', as in 'soon' while the latter is like the vowel sound in 'note'.

'u' pronounced like 'oo' in 'soon'.

Diphthongs

'ai, ei, ay', and 'ey' (pronounced like the diphthong in 'day', though some authorities believe they were sounded like 'i' in 'line'.

'au, aw' pronounced like 'ou' in 'house'; but not before the combination '-ght' like the 'o' in 'not'.

'eu, ew' pronounced like 'ew' in 'few'.

'oi, oy' pronounced like 'oy' in 'boy'.

'ou, ow' pronounced like 'u', or like 'au, aw'.

In words of French origin

Such of these words as had already become part and parcel of the everyday speech would obey the rules for the pronunciation of English vowel sounds; the others would retain the vowels of the French language, which were sounded much as they are today.

In unaccented syllables

The final '-e' so common at the end of a line and elsewhere is sounded like the second syllable of the word 'china'.

Consonants

The consonants had generally the same pronunciation as they have today, with certain slight modifications.

There were no silent consonants, unless, as some scholars believe, the 'g' before 'n' is not sounded.

'kn' is pronounced as in Modern German.

'gg' is pronounced like the 'dge' in Modern English 'ridge'.

'gh' as in Modern German may be either palatal or guttural, according to whether it is preceded by a palatal or a guttural vowel.

'ng' is sounded as in southern English 'fin-ger', not as in 'sing-er'.

'th' (initial) is sounded as in 'thin', not as in 'then'.

'ch' in words of both English and French origin is pronounced like the 'ch' of modern English 'choose'.

'w' before 'r' is pronounced like a rapidly sounded 'oo'.

'h' in words of French origin and in words like 'he, him', which are rarely emphasized, is silent; but in most words of English origin an initial 'h' is sounded. Where the metre demands that a final '-e' should be elided before an 'h', that 'h' is silent.

Final 'f' is sounded as 'f', and not as 'v'.

Final 's' is sounded as 's', and not as 'z'.

Chaucer's use of the final -e

It is important to say something about the function of the final -e found at the end of many words in Chaucer's verse. At the beginning of the fourteenth century these were generally sounded as separate syllables, but by the end of the century they were coming into disuse. In Chaucer's verse the final -e may represent an inflexional change in a noun, an adjective, or a verb; or it may be what is left of a word-ending in Old English. There are many explanations of this termination, and the following rules usually apply in Chaucer.

1 The final -e is usually sounded, except when
(a) it is slurred over before a word beginning with a vowel (e.g. Of deerne love he koude and of solas): before certain words beginning with 'h'; any part of the verb to have (e.g. a clerkhadde litherly biset his while); the adverbs heer, how, and a silent 'h' as in honour, him and hem (e.g. For for no cry hir maide koudehim calle).
(b) it is sometimes dropped in some words in common use as were, wolde.

2 The final -e should always be sounded at the end of a line.

Versification

In earlier works Chaucer had used the eight-syllabled line commonly found in French poets of the period. In the *Canterbury Tales*, however, he sometimes employs the ten-syllabled line, rhyming in couplets. This is his metre throughout the *Pardoner's Tale*. As the line is somewhat long, he made use of a break, or caesura, in the middle of the line, that is after the fifth syllable; but as such a break in every line at the same point would make for a rigidity which would not be in keeping with the easy style of this tale, and of some others, we find the break in other positions. Line 463 has the caesura after the fifth syllable, line 464 after the fourth; 470 after the sixth. Some lines have eleven syllables, as 484, for the final -e is sounded in *dronkenesse*; others have nine only, as 502.

In counting the syllables in a line, we should not forget that when the final -e of one word comes before an initial vowel or -h of a following word, that final -e is elided, that is, it does not count as a syllable: otherwise it is so counted. *-ed* and *-es* are normally sounded separately, while the endings *-ioun*, and *-ience* are dissyllables and trisyllables respectively. When a line ends in a final *-e*, that line contains eleven syllables: it will rhyme with another line of eleven syllables.

General questions

1 'The Pardoner may be corrupt but he is also fascinating.'
Discuss.

Outline of points to cover in your answer

The Pardoner is profoundly corrupt – without redeeming
features, without any sense of remorse, except, arguably, for few
lines at end of poem where he advocates penitence (lines 916–8).
He perverts aim of religious teaching while sheltering under
'umbrella' provided by church (though papal 'bulls' and seals he
shows to congregations may not be genuine), he lives in
deliberate contradiction to Christian principles and delights in
being a 'ful vicious man' and claims with pride,

'I wol noon of the Apostles countrefete'

Our sense of his corruption deepened by fact that it is so evident
to Pardoner himself – he knows the best and chooses the worst,
can tell 'a moral tale' yet behaves worse than any of the villains in
that tale (revellers, at least, aren't hypocritical in their appetites).
In short, Pardoner is completely unscrupulous – lies, defrauds,
preys on simple and poor, loves his own rottenness!
   Despite all this, he is one of most interesting and entertaining
of Canterbury pilgrims. This is partly because flamboyantly 'evil'
characters who make no attempt to conceal wickedness are often
intrinsically attractive to reader/audience. We are let into Pardoner's secrets by the man himself and, however reprehensible
they may be, there's almost a sense of 'privilege', on hearing
information denied to the outside world. There is as well the
interest of learning his technique – false relics, gestures
employed in preaching – and listening to an example of his
sermon. Above all, there is the fascination of the completeness
of self-revelation. Pardoner holds nothing back in his 'confes-
sion' and, just as he holds his congregation with dramatized
treatment of sin and death, so he holds Canterbury pilgrims
with a dynamic treatment of his favourite subject – the dramatiz-
ation of himself.

2 What connection do you see between the attack on sins (lines 483–659) and the story in *The Pardoner's Tale*?

3 'The Pardoner damns himself. There is no need of any condemnation from outside.' Do you agree?

4 Discuss and illustrate the techniques used by the Pardoner in his preaching.

5 What picture of medieval life do we gain from Prologue and Tale?

6 Describe and account for the characterization of the three 'revellers'.

7 What significance has the old man in the Pardoner's narrative?

8 What part do the minor characters – innkeeper, servant, apothecary – play in *The Pardoner's Tale*?

9 'A sombre story utterly unrelieved by humour or human kindness.' Do you agree with this verdict on the story told by the Pardoner?

10 Would you have been convinced by this sermon? Give reasons for your answer.

11 Discuss and give examples of the use of irony in this poem.

12 'A bare but brutally effective piece of work.' Is this a fair assessment of the Pardoner's preaching?'

13 Would you agree that in *The Pardoner's Tale* Chaucer gives us little or no idea of his own convictions, and keeps his own feelings in the background?

14 Give some account of the Pardoner's behaviour towards his fellow-pilgrims at the end of his 'sermon'.

15 How far do you feel that it would be correct to claim that the Pardoner is really attracted to what he condemns?

16 Imagine that you are a Canterbury pilgrim listening to *The Pardoner's Prologue and Tale*. Write a letter (in modern English!) to a friend describing your reaction.

17 How far would you agree that Death could be considered a principal character in *The Pardoner's Tale*?

18 Discuss and give examples of Chaucer's poetic versatility.

19 In what ways might the poem be regarded as an attack on corruption within the church?

20 Why should we continue to read *The Pardoner's Prologue and Tale*?

Further reading

For Chaucer's life and material on *The Canterbury Tales* as a whole see

Geoffrey Chaucer of England Marchette Chute (1946, reissued 1977)

The Life and Times of Chaucer John Gardner (1977)

on *The Pardoner's Prologue and Tale* see

An Introduction to Chaucer Derek Brewer (1984)

Chaucer the Maker John Speirs (1951)

Chaucer: Modern Essays in Criticism ed. Edward Wagenknecht (for the essay 'The Progress of Chaucer's Pardoner, 1880–1940' by G. C. Sedgewick) 1959.

Glossary

Note: Chaucer uses *i* and *y* as equivalents; *ou* and *ow* are interchangeable; as are *-ey-* and *-ay-* (which may also be writen *-ei-* or *-ai-*).

The student is advised to consult the Textual notes in association with this Glossary.

Lines 669–714

affyle *soften, smooth, put an edge on.*

alderbeste *best of all.*

ape *ape, dupe* (l.706).

atte laste *at the last, finally* (l.707).

bare *uncovered, bareheaded* (l.683).

biforn *before, in front* (l.686).

bretful *brimful* (l.687).

burdoun *accompaniment, droning sound* (l.673).

colpon *shred, bundle, hank* (l.679).

compeer *bosom friend, comrade* (l.670).

craft *profession, professional skill* (l.692).

croys *cross* (l.699).

dischevele *with untidy hair* (l.683).

ecclesiaste *preacher* (l.708).

eye *eye* (l.152).

feyne *pretend* (l.705).

flex *flax* (l.676).

gelding *gelding* (l.691).

gentil *well-disposed, kindly* (l.669).

gobet *piece, fragment* (l.696).

goot *goat* (l.688).

hangen *hang* (l.677).

henten *seize, catch* (l.698).

hider *hither* (l.672).

hoot *hot* (l.687).

jape *jest, trick, trickery* (l.705).

jet *fashion, style* (l.682).

jolitee *fun, bravado* (l.680).

latoun *brass* (l.699). See note.

lokke *lock, curl* (l.677).

male *bag, wallet* (l.694).

moste *must, would have to* (l.712).

offertorie (l.710). See note.

oon *one* (l.679).

ounce *small piece, bunch* (l.677).

oversprede *spread over, cover* (l.678).

person *parson, clergyman* (l.702).

pig *pig* (l.700).

pilwe-beer *pillow-case* (l.694).

relik *relic* (l.701).

see *sea, water* (l.698).

seyl *sail* (l.696).

shulder *shoulder* (l.678).

somnour *summoner, one who summons another to an ecclesiastical court* (l.673).

soun *sound, noise* (l.674).

stone *stone* (l.699).

storie *story* (l.709). See note.

strike *hank of flax* (l.676).

swich *such,* (l.684).

trowe *suppose, believe, should say* (l.691).

tweye *two, twain* (l.704).

up on lond *far in the country, off the beaten track* (l.702).

vernicle *vernicle* (l.685). See note.

veyl *veil* (l.695).

walet *scrip, bag* (l.681).

wente *walked* (l.697).
wex *wax, beeswax* (l.675).
wiste *knew* (l.711).

Lines 287–968

a *on.* See **a-paas,** (l.866).
abhominable *abominable* (l.471, 631).
ablakeberyed *blackberrying, astray* (l.406).
abought *purchased* (l.503).
abye *purchased, paid for* (l.756).
accident *that which is accidental* (l.539).
actes *histories, records* (l.574).
adoun *down* (l.925).
adversarie *adversary, enemy* (l.682).
advocat *advocate, counsel* (l.291).
agayn *against* (l.427).
agayns *in the presence of* (l.743).
agon *past, gone, ago* (l.610).
al *all* (l.336).
al *although* (l.449, 451).
alle *all* (l.574).
alday *continually* (l.294).
ale-stake *ale-stake* (l.321). See note.
algate *at any rate, however* (l.292).
almost *almost* (l.313).
al-so *just as* (l.860).
alliaunce *alliance* (l.605).
allone *alone* (l.841).
allye *ally* (l.613).
alwey *always, continually* (l.333).
amende *reform, correct* (l.767).
amis *wrongly* (l.642).
annex *attach, link with* (l.482).
anon *at once, immediately* (l.316, 319, 357, 477).
a-pass *slowly, at walking pace* (l.866).
appetyt *appetite* (l.546).
armes *arms* (l.654).
artow *(contraction for) art thou* (l.552, 718).

aryse *arise, stand up* (l.744).
as *as if* (l.287).
assent *party, plot* (l.758).
assoille *pardon, absolve* (l.387, 913, 939).
asterte *escape, avoid* (l.414).
atte *(contraction for) at the* (l.608).
atwo *in two* (l.677, 936).
auctoritee *authority* (l.387).
avaryce *avarice, greed* (l.400).
avaunce *advance, benefit* (l.410).
aventure *adventure, danger, peril* (l.934).
avow *boast, vow* (l.695).
avyse *warn, consider, advise* (l.583, 690).
awey *away, aside* (l.542).
axe *ask* (l.667).
ay *continually* (l.554, 581).
bad *bade* (l.803).
baskettes *baskets* (l.375).
baud *bawd, procurer* (l.479).
be *to be.*
beautee *beauty* (l.293, 839).
been *are* (l.472, 617, 774).
beggen *beg* (l.446).
bekke *nod, beckon with the head* (l.396).
bel-amy *good friend* (l.318).
bely *belly* (l.534).
bere *bear, carry* (l.915).
berie *bury* (l.884).
berne *barn* (l.397).
beestes *beasts, animals* (l.361).
bet *quickly* (l.667).
beth *be.*
beye *buy* (l.845).
bicched *cursed* (l.656).
bicomen *become* (l.698).
bidde *bid, ask* (l.803).
bifore *before, previously* (l.880).
biforn *in front of* (l.665, 707).
biginne *begin* (l.941).
biholde *behold, see, observe* (l.639).
bisinesse *business, briskness* (l.399).
bitide *happen, befall, come about* (l.900).

bitwix *between* (l.494).

biwreye *reveal, proclaim, expose* (l.823).

blakeberyed *blackberrying*: see line 406, and note.

blaspheme *blasphemy* (l.593).

blasphemour *blasphemer, one who speaks profanely,* (l.898).

blede *to bleed* (l.581).

blisse *blessedness, bliss* (l.912).

blissed *blessed* (l.474).

blowe *kindle, blow* (l.481).

blythe *glad, happy* (l.795).

body *body* (l.474).

boght *bought* (l.501).

boghte *bought* (l.766).

boke *book* (l.630).

bone *bone* (l.656).

boon *bone* (l.350).

boost *boast, boasting* (l.764).

born *born* (l.915).

borwe *borrow* (l.871).

botel *bottle* (l.871).

bourde *jest* (l.778).

bowen *bend, bow* (l.909).

boy *boy, page, servant* (l.670).

boyste *box* (l.307).

breech *breeches* (l.948).

breed *bread* (l.797).

breeth *breath* (l.552).

breke *break* (l.936).

brighte *bright, shining* (l.774).

broches *brooches* (l.908).

broghte *brought* (l.802).

bulle *Papal Bull, edict, document* (l.336).

busshels *bushels* (l.771).

but *unless* (l.314, 741).

by *close, near* (l.566).

by *by, during, by means of* (l.288, 858, 458).

cake *loaf of unsweetened bread* (l.322). See note.

callen *call* (l.666).

cam *came* (l.606).

canon See note on line 890.

capitayn *captain* (l.582).

capoun *domestic fowl* (l.856).

cardynacle See note on line 313.

cardiacle See **cardynacle,** *above.*

carie *carry, transfer* (l.800).

carl *fellow, churl* (l.717).

cas *accident, chance* (l.885).

cast *plan, devise* (l.880).

catel *property, goods* (l.594).

cause *reason* (l.446).

certes *certainly, truly, surely* (l.407).

chambre *room* (l.735).

chaunce *chance* (l.606, 653).

chaunge *exchange, change* (l.724).

cheere *countenance, face, disposition* (l.963).

cherl *fellow, churl, peasant* (l.289, 750).

chese *cheese* (l.448).

cheste *treasure chest* (l.734).

child *child, lad* (l.686).

cleer *clear, bright* (l.914).

clene *clean, pure* (l.873).

clepe *call, name* (l.675).

clerk *scholar, clergyman* (l.339, 391).

clinke *tinkle* (l.664).

clout *piece of cloth* (l.348).

cod *bag, belly* (l.534).

cok *cock* (l.362).

cokewold *husband of a faithless wife* (l.382).

come *come* (l.910, 925).

comaund *command* (l.584).

commune *common, general,* (l.596).

compaignye *company, group* (l.463).

conclusion *conclusion, ending* (l.454).

confiture *preparation* (l.862).

confusion *downfall, destruction* (l.499).

conseil *secret, secrecy* (l.561, 819).

contrarie *opposite* (l.595).

contree *country, native land, district, neighbourhood,* (l.610, 676, 754).

cooke *cook* (l.538).

corn *grain* (l.863).

corny *strong, with plenty of body* (l.315, 456).

corpus *the Body of Christ* (l.314). See note.

correccioun *correction, admonition* (l.404).

corrupcioun *corruption, foulness* (l.535).

corrupt *corrupt, depraved, debased* (l.504).

cors *body, corpse* (l.304, 665).

countrefete *copy, imitate* (l.447).

coveityse *covetousness, greed* (l.424).

crepe *creep* (l.565).

croked *crooked, winding* (l.761).

crowe *crow* (l.362).

croys *cross* (l.532).

cure *care, interest, concern* (l.557).

curs *curse* (l.946).

cursednesse *wickedness, evil practices* (l.400).

curteisye *act of courtesy, courteous manners* (l.739).

cut *lot, the shortest straw* (l.793).

cynk *five* (l.653).

dame *lady, mother* (l.684).

dampnable *damnable, outrageous* (l.472).

dampnacioun *condemnation* (l.500).

dar *dare, venture* (l.297, 380, 574).

daunce *dance* (l.467).

debate *contend, attack, quarrel* (l.412).

deceite *deception, deceit* (l.592).

deceyve *deceive.*

dede *deed, actually* (l.525).

deed *dead* (l.548).

deere *dear, beloved* (l.301).

deere *dearly, at high price* (l.293, 502).

dees *dice* (l.834).

deeth *death* (l.533, 675).

defame *infamy, loss of reputation,*

dishonour (l.612).

defame *slander, dishonour* (l.415).

defaute *fault, sin, default* (l.370).

deffende *forbid* (l.510, 590).

delices *delights, pleasures* (l.547).

delyt *delight* (l.545). See note.

depart *share, divide* (l.812).

desolaat *abandoned morally* (l.598).

destourbe (see **distourbe**).

destroye *destroy* (l.523, 858).

devel *devil* (l.469).

devocioun *devotion, adoration* (l.346).

devyse *invent, devise, think of* (l.290, 423).

deyde *died* (l.580).

deyntee *delicate, out of the ordinary* (l.520).

diete *diet, eating* (l.516).

digne *worthy, honourable, venerable* (l.695).

dignitee *honour, worthiness* (l.701, 782).

discrecioun *discretion, judgement, prudence* (l.559).

dishonour *dishonour* (l.691).

displesance *annoyance, what displeases* (l.420).

distourbe *disturb, interfere with, hinder* (l.340).

dominacioun *rule, control, power, mastery* (l.560).

donge *dung* (l.535).

doom *judgement, justice* (l.637).

doon *do, cause, bring about* (l.790).

doost (l.312).

dooth *does* (l.397).

doun *down* (l.392).

doute *doubt* (l.822).

douteless *without doubt, indeed, truly* (l.492).

dowve *dove, pigeon* (l.397).

draught *draught, drink* (l.315).

drawe *draw, come* (l.966).

drede *doubt* (l.507).

drinke *drink* (l.363 etc.).

drank *drank* (l.555).

dronken *drunk* (l.568).

dronke *drunk* (l.456, 862).

dronkelewe *habitually drunk* (l.495). See note.

dronkenesse *drunkenness* (l.484, 549).

dryve *drive, cause to pass, while away* (l.628).

dyen *die* (l.615, 703).

ech *each* (l.697).

echoon *each one* (l.349).

eek *also* (l.306).

eighte *eight* (l.771).

eir *air* (l.519).

eldre *older* (l.364).

eldres *elders, ancestors* (l.364).

elles *otherwise, else* (l.315).

embassadour *ambassador* (l.603).

empoisoning *poisoning* (l.891).

empoysonere *poisoner* (l.894).

ende *end* (l.533).

ende *come to an end, perish* (l.893).

ending *end, close* (l.892).

ensample *example, illustrative stories* (l.435).

entencioun *intent, purpose* (l.408).

entente *intention* (l.403, 849).

entre *enter, insert, record* (l.91).

envoluped *wrapped up* (l.942).

er *before* (l.362, 671).

erly *early* (l.730).

erme *grieve, sorrow, mourn* (l.312).

erst *first of all* (l.662). See note.

erthe *earth* (l.519).

espye *spy* (l.755).

est *east* (l.396).

estaat *rank, condition* (l.597).

eten *eat* (l.458).

everich *each* (l.768).

everichon *every one* (l.944).

expresly *definitely, explicitly* (l.536).

ey *what!* (l.782).

fader *father, ancestor* (l.505).

falle *fall, occur*.

fil *fell* (l.804).

fals *false, untrue* (l.903).

fame *evil report* (l.385).

famyne *famine, hunger* (l.451).

faste *close, near* (l.566).

fastynge *fasting* (l.363).

fayn *gladly, eagerly* (l.857).

feend *devil, Satan* (l.844).

feeste *feast, banquet* (l.489).

feith *faith, word* (l.524).

felawe *comrade, companion* (l.672).

felaweship *comradeship, companionship* (l.938).

felicitee *happiness* (l.787).

fen *section of a book, chapter* (l.890).

fest *fist* (l.802).

fetys *slender, slim, dainty, shapely* (l.478).

fey *faith, word* (l.762).

fil *see* falle.

finden *find, discover, provide for* (l.627).

fond *found* (l.608).

flaterye *flattery* (l.409).

floryn *florin* (l.770). See note.

folwe *follow*.

folwen *follow* (l.514).

folye *foolish practice, folly* (l.464).

for *because* (l.440, 443).

for *because of* (l.433).

for to *in order to* (l.346).

forbede *forbid*.

forbade (l.633).

forbedeth (l.643).

forby *close by* (l.668).

for-dronke *dead-drunk* (l.674).

forgat *forgot* (l.919).

forlete *lose* (l.864).

fors *matter, consequence* (l.303).

forswering *perjury, false swearing* (l.592, 657).

forthermo *furthermore, moreover* (l.594).

fortherover *furthermore, moreover* (l.648).

forwhy *because* (l.847).

forwrapped *closely wrapped* (l.718).

foryete *forget*.

foryeve *forgive* (l.904).

free *generous, liberal* (l.401).

freed *friend* (l.832).

fro *from* (l.506).

fruyt *fruit* (l.510).

frutesteres *fruit-girls* (l.478). See note. to l.477.

ful *full* (l.307).

ful *full, very* (l.300, 459, 491, 529).

fulfille *filled full* (l.535, 540).

fumositee *heavy vapour, headiness* (l.567).

fyne *fine, pure* (l.770).

fyr *fire* (l.481).

galianes See note to l.306.

gan *began. Also used as an auxiliary meaning 'did'* (l.287, 323, 666).

gaude *trick* (l.389).

gentil *noble* (l.304).

gentils *gentlefolk, my lords* (l.383).

gete *get, procure for* (l.520).

giltelees *innocent, blameless* (l.491).

gilty *guilty* (l.429).

glorie *glory, fame, honour* (l.625).

glotonye *gluttony* (l.482, 897).

glotoun *glutton* (l.520).

go *go, walk* (l.543, 748).

goon *gone* (l.389, 706, 711).

Goddes (l.386).

golet *gullet, throat* (l.543).

goode-man *master of the house* (l.361).

governaunce *rule, government* (l.600).

grace *favour* (l.383, 783, 717).

graunte *agree, grant* (l.327, 388, 822).

grayn *grain, seed,* (l.374).

greet *great, excessive* (l.472, 612).

grette *greet* (l.714).

grettest *greatest* (l.607).

grinde *grind* (l.538).

grisly *dreadful, horrible, terrifying* (l.473, 708).

grote *a coin, worth fourpence in Chaucer's days* (l.376, 945).

grove *grove* (l.762).

gytern *a musical instrument, guitar* (l.467).

habitacioun *dwelling* (l.689).

han *have* (l.300, 330, 393, 587, 725).

hadde *had* (l.815).

happe *happen* (l.606, 885).

harp *harp* (l.466).

harrow *help!* (l.288).

hasard *a game with dice, gambling* (l.465, 591).

hasardour *gambler* (l.751).

hasardrye *gambling* (l.590).

haunte *practise, devote oneself to* (l.464).

hauteyn *lofty, elevated, high-pitched* (l.330).

hawe *farmyard, enclosure* (l.855).

heed *head* (l.743, 909).

heer *here.*

heere *hear* (l.302, 473).

herd *heard* (l.393).

heeste *behest, order, commandment* (l.490, 640).

heigh *high, great* (l.633, 787, 913).

hele *heal, cure* (l.366).

hem *them* (l.308, 401, 435).

henne *hence* (l.687).

hente *take, seize* (l.868).

herkne *listen, hearken.*

herkneth *listen* (l.454, 573, 696).

herte *heart* (l.290, 312).

hewe *colour, pretence* (l.421).

heyre-clout *hair-cloth* (l.736).

hir *her* (l.370).

hir, hire *their* (l.291, 402, 468, 533, 605).

his *his, its* (l.665).

holde *retain in memory* (l.438); *keep,* (l.462); *esteem* (l.596, 598).

holynesse *piety, goodness* (l.422).

homicyde *manslaughter* (l.644).

homicyde *murderer* (l.893).

honeste *respectable, decent* (l.328, 557).

honge *hang* (l.790). See note.

honour *reputation, moral worth* (l.617).

honurable *honourable, to be honoured* (l.640).

hool *whole, healed* (l.357).

hooly *holy* (l.340).

hoom *home* (l.569, 610).

hoor *hoary, white* (l.743).

hoord *hoard* (l.775).

hous *house* (l.649).

hyer *higher, more exalted* (l.597).

hym *him, himself* (l.475, 610).

hyne *servant, labourer* (l.688).

ich *I*. See note to l.947.

jalous *jealous* (l.367).

jalousye *jealousy* (l.366).

jape *jest, trick* (l.319, 394).

joliftee *jollity, happiness, gaiety* (l.780).

joly *jolly, merry, lively* (l.453).

juge *judge* (l.291).

justise *judge, law* (l.289).

kaityf *captive, wretch* (l.728).

kan *know, be able* (l.332, 427).

kanstow *canst thou* (l.521).

keepe *notice, heed* (l.352, 360, 777).

kepe *keep, guard, take care of* (l.561, 562, 798).

kindle *kindle, set alight* (l.481).

kisse *kiss, embrace* (l.968).

knave *boy, attendant, servant* (l.666).

knele *kneel* (l.925).

knokke *knock* (l.541).

knowe *know* (l.646).

labour *work, toil* (l.444, 506).

lafte *left* (l.762).

lasse *less, inferior* (l.602, 865, 939).

latoun *brass* (l.350).

laughe *laugh* (l.967).

leche *healer, physician* (l.916).

lecherye *debauchery, love of luxury* (l.481).

leef *eager, desirous* (l.760).

leef *leaf* (l.544).

leere *learn* (l.325, 578).

leet *let, allow, permit* (l.731).

leeve *dear* (l.731).

lenger *longer* (l.497).

lese *lose, forfeit* (l.611).

lete *forsake, leave, permit* (l.659).

letuarie *medicinal powders* (l.307). See note.

lesyng *lie, falsehood* (l.591).

leve *leave, permission* (l.848).

leve *leave, give up*.

lafte *left* (762).

levere *rather, more desirable* (l.615).

lewed *ignorant, base, ill-educated* (l.392, 437).

licour *liquor, juice* (l.452).

lige *liege, feudal* (l.337).

lightly *easily, quickly* (l.752).

likerous *wanton, lustful* (l.540).

looke *look, take care* (l.579, 621, 669).

lond *land* (l.607).

longe *long* (l.436).

lordings *gentlemen, sirs, my masters* (l.329).

lough *laugh* (l.476, 961).

love *love, enjoy* (l.437).

lust *desires, delights* (l.833).

luxurie *gluttony, lust* (l.484, 897).

lye *lie, speak falsely* (l.636).

lyf *life* (l.727, 780).

lyk *like* (l.310, 728).

lyking *desire, wish* (l.455, 458).

lyven *live, spend* (l.780).

lyvestow *livest thou* (l.719).

lyvynge *manner of life* (l.847).

maister *master* (l.301).

maken *make* (l.368, 382).

maladye *illness, sickness, disease* (l.513).

male *bag, wallet* (l.920).

maner *kind, sort, manner* (l.627). See note.

manslaughtre *manslaughter* (l.593).

mark *mark, a coin worth forty groats.*

mary *marrow from bones* (l.542).

matere *matter, subject* (l.434).

may *may, can* (l.325, 372, 439, 710, 758, 816).

mayde *maiden, girl* (l.292).

mekely *humbly* (l.926).

merie *merry.*

mesurable *moderate, within bounds* (l.515).

mete *food (not necessarily flesh food)* (l.520).

mitayn, miteyn *mitten, glove* (l.372, 373).

mo *more* (l.678).

montance *amount, quantity* (l.863).

moodor *mother* (l.729, 731).

moore *more* (l.939).

moore *more* (l.369).

moot *must* (l.309, 327, 725).

moste *must* (l.791).

mowe *can* (l.932).

moyste *freshly brewed* (l.315).

multiplye *increase, multiply* (l.365).

multiplying *increase* (l.374).

murie *merry* (l.843).

myght *power, capacity* (l.468).

myghte *might* (l.792, 840, 846).

myrie *merry* (l.316).

myrthe *pleasure, amusement, something amusing* (l.319).

mystriste *mistrust* (l.369).

name *name, reputation* (l.611).

namely *particularly, especially* (l.402, 563).

namoore *no more* (l.588, 684).

nat *not* (l.311, 403, 571).

natheles *nevertheless* (l.303, 813).

nayles *nails* (l.288, 651). See notes to these lines.

ne *not* (l.745); *nor* (l.383).

ne . . . ne *neither . . . nor* (l.339).

necessarie *necessary, needful* (l.681).

nede *to be necessary* (l.670).

neer *nearer* (l.966).

nekke *neck* (l.395).

neveradel *not at all* (l.670).

nexte *nearest* (l.870).

newe *again* (l.929).

noble *a coin , worth twenty groats, or half a mark* (l.907).

noght *not at all* (l.417, 475).

noght *nothing at all* (l.542).

noon *none* (l.412, 447).

noot *don't* (l.816).

nothyng *in no way, not at all* (l.404, 433, 764).

nothyng *nothing* (l.424).

ny *nearly* (l.771).

o *one* (l.377).

of *of* (l.315, 374); *because of* (l.317); *from* (l.356, 408, 449, 450, 936); *away from* (l.340).

officere *officer, servant* (l.480).

offren *offer, make offering of* (l.910).

ofte-tyme *often, frequently* (l.408).

oght *behoves, is our duty* (l.434, 512).

old *old, aged* (l.436, 713, 720, 750).

on *at, against* (l.512).

ones *of one mind, in agreement* (l.696).

ook *oak-tree* (l.765).

oon *one, the same* (l.333).

ooth *oath.*

ordre *order, place on the list* (l.645).

original *origin, source* (l.500).

ote *oat* (l.375).

othe *oath* (472, 629, 636, 708).

other *other* (l.476).

otherweys *in any other way* (l.412).

oures *ours* (l.786).

out *out, aloud* (l.331, 421).

out-cast *cast out, expelled* (l.511).

outrageous *violent, unrestrained* (l.650).

outrely *indeed, in truth* (l.849).

over *more* (l.648).

overal *in addition to* (l.583).

owen *own* (l.361, 490, 790).

owe *own* (l.361).

oxe *ox* (l.354).

paas *pace, walking pace* (l.866).

page *servant, attendant* (l.449, 688).

pale *pale, pallid* (l.738).

par cas *by chance* (l.885).

par chaunce *as it happened* (l.106).

pardee *by heaven* (l.672).

parten *depart* (l.649, 752).

passe *pass* (l.303, 940).

patente *letter of privilege to ask alms of the faithful* (l.337).

pees *peace, silence* (l.462).

peny *penny; pl. pens* (l.376).

peple *people* (l.392, 437).

peraventure *by chance* (l.935).

persevere *last, continue* (l.497).

peyne *pain, torment* (l.511).

peyne *take pains, endeavour* (330, 395).

pitee *pity, sorrow, distress* (l.317).

pitous *piteous, pitiful,* (l.302, 531).

pitously *piteously* (l.298, 529).

plat *plainly* (l.648).

plentee *plenty, amount, quantity* (l.811).

plesaunce *pleasure, amusement* (l.409).

pley *play, pastime* (l.627).

pleye *play, play about* (l.467, 608, 778, 827).

pleyne *complain, lament, grieve* (l.512).

plight *pledged* (l.702).

pokkes *eruptions on the face, pimples* (l.358).

polcat *polecat, weasel* (l.855).

policye *policy, administration, public business* (l.600).

potage *soup, stew* (l.368).

pothecarie *apothecary, herbalist* (l.852).

poverte *poverty* (l.441).

povereste *poorest* (l.449).

povre *poor* (l.713).

poyson *poison* (l.845, 854).

preche *preach* (l.393, 427).

preching *discourse, sermon* (l.401, 414).

predicacioun *discourse, sermon* (l.345, 407).

preest *priest* (l.371).

prelat *priest, prelate* (l.310).

prey *beg, pray, implore* (l.965).

preyere *prayer* (l.577).

prime *prime, the first service of the day* (l.662). See note.

privee *secret, stealthy* (l.675).

prively *secretly, stealthily* (l.797).

pronounce *announce* (l.335).

propre *real, actual, handsome* (l.309, 417).

proud *bold* (l.716).

prow *profit, advantage, benefit* (l.300).

pulpet *pulpit* (l.391).

purs *purse, money bag* (l.945).

putte *put, place,* (l.373, 845).

quelle *kill* (l.854).

quod *quoth, said* (l.288).

quyte *requite, pay back, punish* (l.420).

rage *rage, fury* (l.367, 705).

rather *earlier, sooner* (l.643).

ratt *rat* (l.854).

receyve *receive* (l.926).

rede *red* (l.562).

rede *advise* (l.941).

rede *read* (l.508).

redily *quickly, without delay* (l.667).

redy *ready, on the alert* (l.683).

reed *advice, counsel* (l.744).

rekke *care* (l.405).

relik *relic* (l.349).

rende *tear, rend* (l.475).

renne *run* (l.796).

renoun *renown, repute* (l.625).

repaire *return, go back* (l.878).

repente *repent* (l.431).

replet *full* (l.489).

reporte *relate, narrate* (l.438, 669).

reprevable *worthy of reproof,*

shameful (l.632).

repreeve *reproach, shame* (l.595).

resoun *opinion, reason* (l.458). See note.

restelees *restless* (l.728).

ribaudye *ribaldry, debauchery* (l.324).

right *just, very* (l.490, 583, 753).

rightwisnesse *righteousness* (l.637).

ringe *ring, resound* (l.331).

rong (l.662).

riot *revelry, debauchery, gambling* (l.465).

riotour *reveller, gambler* (l.661, 692).

rolle *roll, document* (l.911).

rolle *consider, turn over in one's mind* (l.838).

roote *root* (l.544).

rote *heart, rote, memory* (l.332).

round *evenly, smoothly, continuously* (l.331, 770).

ryde *ride* (l.748).

ryng *ring* (l.908).

ryve *stab, thrust.*

sacrifyse *sacrifice* (l.469).

saffron *flavour, colour* (l.345).

sauce *sauce* (l.545).

saugh *saw* (l.961).

sayn *say* (l.297).

   seith (l.492).

   seyde *said* (l.311).

scabbe *scab* (l.358).

see *see, note with favour* (l.294, 372, 715).

seel *seal of authority* (l.337).

seken *seek.*

selle *sell* (l.564).

sely *innocent* (l.292).

semen *seem, appear* (l.422, 553).

sende *send* (l.614).

sepulture *grave, tomb* (l.558).

sermone *to preach a sermon, to discourse* (l.879).

sette *sit down* (l.392, 775, 826).

seuretee *security* (l.937).

seye *say* (l.294, 574).

seyn *say* (l.789, 819).

shal *shall, must, ought to* (l.320, 359, 618, 733, 825).

   sholde *shoulder* (l.457, 616).

shamful *dreadful, shameful, ignominious* (l.290).

shape *prepare, get ready, intend.*

   shoop *intended* (l.874).

sheep *sheep* (l.354).

sholde see shal.

sholder *shoulder* (l.350).

shoop see shape.

shrewe *scoundrel, villain* (l.496, 819).

shul see shal.

sighte *sight* (l.773).

signe *sign, symptom* (l.419).

sire *master, sir* (l.366).

sith *afterwards, then* (l.869).

sith *since* (l.390).

sitte *sit* (l.664, 674, 883).

   sat (l.664, 674).

sleen *slay, kill* (l.491).

   sleeth *slays* (l.676).

   slaw *killed* (l.856).

slyly *stealthily, secretly* (l.792).

smale *small, slender* (l.478).

smerte *smartly, severely, painfully* (l.413).

smyte *strike, smite.*

   smoot (l.677).

sobrenesse *sobriety* (l.582)).

sodeynly *suddenly* (l.673).

softe *softly, gently, easily* (l.543).

soghte *sought* (l.488).

som *some* (l.325).

sondry *different, various* (l.443).

sone *soon* (l.609).

soor *sore* (l.358).

soore *sorely, with sorrow* (l.431).

sooth *truly* (l.636).

soothly *truly* (l.758).

sorwe *sorrow* (l.848).

sory *sad, sorrowful, unlucky* (l.717, 876).

soule *soul* (l.406, 916).

soun *sound* (l.553).

sovereyn *supreme, most notable* (l.574).

sowe *sow* (l.375).

special *special, particular* (l.634).

speke *speak* (l.740).

  spak *spoke* (l.753, 807).

  y-spoke *spoke* (l.589).

spere *spear* (l.677).

spicerye *spices, spicery* (l.544).

spitte *spit* (l.421).

spoon *spoon* (l.908).

staf *staff, stick* (l.730).

stele *steal, go secretly.*

stampe *pound in a mortar* (l.538).

sterling *silver penny* (l.907).

sterve *die, put to death,* (l.451, 865, 888).

stike *stab, stick* (l.556).

stille *continually, for ever* (l.725).

stinge *sting* (l.413).

stirte *start, jump* (l.705).

stire *stir, incite* (l.346).

stonde *stand* (l.391).

stoon *precious stone* (l.347). See note.

stoor *store, dead stock* (l.365).

storie *story, history, record* (l.488).

strecche *stretch* (l.395).

strenger *stronger* (l.825).

strete *street, paved way* (l.694).

streyne *strain through a sieve* (l.538).

strogel *struggle* (l.829).

strong *powerful, effective, virulent* (l.867).

stryving *strife, contention* (l.550).

stywe *brothel, house of bad reputation* (l.465).

substaunce *substance, real nature* (l.539). See note.

subtilly *in subtle fashion, cunningly* (l.565, 798).

suffisant *capable, adequate* (l.932).

suffyse *be sufficient, suffice* (l.588).

superfluitee *excess, excesses* (l.471, 528).

swelle *swell* (l.354).

swere *swear* (l.473, 949).

  sworne (l.808).

switch *such* (l.383, 400).

swinke *toil, work hard* (l.874).

swithe *quickly* (l.796).

swoote *sweetly* (l.543).

swyn *pig* (l.556).

syde *side* (l.828).

synne *sin* (l.379).

take *take* (l.352, 360, 642).

talent *craving, desire, appetite* (l.540).

tarie *delay* (l.799, 851).

tassoile = *to* **assoille** *absolve, give absolution* (l.933).

taverner *innkeeper* (l.685).

teche *teach* (l.440).

telle *tell, relate.*

  toold (l.530, 671).

tendre *tender* (l.517).

terme *formal language, set terms* (l.311).

thanne *then* (l.326).

that *that, so that* (l.313, 325).

that *combined with 'which' to make a relative pronoun* (l.351).

thee *prosper, thrive, have good luck* (l.309). **theech** (l.947), *is thee + ich.* = *may I have good luck.*

theef *theif* (l.675, 759, 789).

theme *subject of discourse, topic* (l.333, 425).

ther *where* (l.886).

ther-biforn *formerly, on a previous occasion* (l.624).

therby *by that means, thereby* (l.445).

thider *to that place, thither* (l.749).

thilke *the same* (l.364, 503, 528).

thinken *think.*

  thoghte *thought* (l.442).

thinken *seem* (l.681, 801).

  thoghte *seemed* (l.475, 771).

  thynketh (l.681). See note.

thise *these* (l.835).

tho *those* (l.548).

thridde *third* (l.836).

throte *throat* (l.517, 527).

thrugh *through* (l.469, 553).

thurghout *right through* (l.655).

thyng *subject, thing* (l.328).

til *to* (l.697).

to *too* (l.293, 650).

togidres *together* (l.702).

tombestere *acrobat, tumbler, dancer* (l.477). See note.

tonge *tongue* (l.356, 557).

to-nyght *last night* (l.673). See note.

to-rente *tear to pieces, rend asunder* (l.709).

torn *turn, show of kindness* (l.815).

to-tere *tear to pieces, rend asunder* (l.474).

toun *town* (l.570).

toward *towards* (l.805).

toweardes *towards* (l.706).

traytour *traitorous* (l.896).

tresor *treasure hoard* (l.779).

trespas *wrong, sin* (l.904).

trespasse *do wrong, sin* (l.741).

trespased (l.416).

trete *tell, treat of, deal with* (l.521, 630).

tretee *agreement, treaty* (l.619).

trewe *true, genuine, honest* (l.422).

trewely *truly, certainly, indeed* (l.301, 442).

treye *three* (l.653).

triacle *antidote, cordial, balm* (l.314).

trede *tread*.

troden (l.712).

trone *throne* (l.842).

trouthe *truth, true feeling, troth* (l.615, 702, 755).

trowe *suppose, think* (l.439, 689).

turne *turn, convert, change* (l.539).

tweye *two* (l.817).

twinne *separate, depart* (l.430).

tyme *time, season* (l.436).

unbokele *unbuckle, undo* (l.945).

understonde *understand*.

unkynde *unnatural, hard-hearted* (l.903).

upright *in an upright position* (l.674). See note.

usage *habit, custom, use* (l.899).

use *use, make use of* (l.428).

vanysshe *vanish, waste away* (l.732).

venym *hatred, malice* (l.421).

vermin *stealthy animals* (l.858). See note.

verray *true, truthful, veritable* (l.480, 576).

veyne *vain, empty* (l.411).

vicious *wicked, vicious, immoral* (l.459).

vileinye *wickedness, rudeness, ill-breeding* (l.503, 740).

village *village* (l.450, 687).

visage *face* (l.720).

voys *voice* (l.531).

vice *vice, wickedness* (l.427).

vyne *vine* (l.452).

waferer *confectioner, maker of wafers, seller of cakes* (l.479). See note to l.478.

walke *walk* (l.530).

war *ware, wary, on one's guard* (l.682).

ware *guard* (l.905).

warente *safeguard, ensure safety of* (l.338).

warne *warn against* (l.377).

warice *save, cure, set free* (l.906).

wasshe *wash* (l.353).

wast *waste* (l.593).

weel *well, fully, accurately* (l.669).

welked *withered* (l.738).

welle *well* (l.353).

wenche *wench, girl* (l.453).

wende *go, leave* (l.927).

wene *suppose, imagine, believe* (l.349).

wende *believed* (l.782).

weneth *imagines* (l.569).

wepe *weep*.

wepyng *weeping* (l.529).

wey *road, path* (l.694, 761, 968).
whan *when* (l.329).
what *what?* (l.439, 717).
whennes *whence* (l.335).
wher *where* (l.756).
wheras *where* (l.466).
wherfor *for this reason* (l.744).
whete *wheat* (l.375).
which *what a* (l.937).
which that *which, who* (l.351, 700).
whiles *while* (l.439).
whilom *once upon a time, formerly* (l.463).
whom that *whom* (l.560).
whyl that *while* (l.508).
white *white, white wine* (l.526, 562).
wight *person* (l.378).
wikkednesse *wickedness* (l.896).
wilfully *deliberately, willingly* (l.441).
wille *wish, desire, be willing.*
  wol *will* (l.322, 326).
  wolde *wished* (l.712, 857).
wise *fashion, manner* (l.470).
wite *know, wiste* (l.370, 513).
  woost *know* (l.810).
wit *intelligence, judgement, wit* (l.326, 559).
with-outen *without* (l.678).
witnesse *take as witness* (l.634).
wo *sorrow, distress, misery* (l.506).
wolle *wool* (l.448, 910).
wombe *stomach* (l.522).
wonder *wondrous, wonderful* (l.891).
wone *be accustomed.*
wont (l.461).
wood *mad* (l.287).
woodnesse *madness* (l.496).
woot *knows* (l.555).
worm *snake, reptile* (l.355).
worste *worst, wickedest* (l.776).
worthy *noble* (l.960).
wrappe *wrap* (l.736).
wrecchednesse *misery,*

wretchedness (l.550).
wrecche *wretch* (l.892).
wreke *avenge* (l.857).
wrooth *wroth, angry* (l.957).
wydwe *widow* (l.450).
wyf *woman, wife* (l.369).
wyke *week* (l.362).
wyn *wine* (l.484, 489, 549, 555, 797).
wynne *win, gain* (l.403).
wonne (l.389).
wyn-yevyng *giving of wine* (l.587).
wyse *wise, prudent, far-seeing* (l.603).
y- is the sign of the past participle.
y-bore *born* (l.704).
y-caried *carried* (l.791).
y-coyned *coined* (l.770).
y-crammed *crammed, filled* (l.348).
ydel *idle, vain* (l.638).
ydelly *idly, without result, in vain* (l.446).
ye *yea, indeed* (l.692).
yeer *year* (l.389, 686).
yerne *eagerly, busily, excitedly* (l.398).
yet *always, still* (l.425).
yeve *give* (l.402).
  yaf *gave* (l.490).
  yeven *given* (l.779).
y-granted *grant* (l.388).
y-hent *taken, seized* (l.868).
y-holde *held, considered* (l.602).
yifte *gift* (l.295, 299).
y-maked *made, prepared* (l.382, 545).
ynogh *enough.*
Ynde *India* (l.722).
yong *young* (l.464, 478).
youres *yours* (l.785).
youthe *youth* (l.724).
yow *you* (l.377).
ypocras *hippocras, a wine* (l.306). See note.
ypocrisye *hypocrisy* (l.410).
y-set *seated* (l.392).

y-shriven *absolved, shriven* (l.380).
y-slawe *killed* (l.856).
y-slayn (l.673).

y-spoke *spoken* (l.589).
y-stonge *stung* (l.335).
yvel *evil, wicked* (l.408).
ywis *surely, certainly* (l.327).

Pan study aids <small>Titles published in the Brodie's Notes series</small>

E. Albee Who's Afraid of Virginia Woolf

Jane Austen Emma Pride and Prejudice

Anthologies of Poetry The Metaphysical Poets

Stan Barstow A Kind of Loving & Joby

Robert Bolt A Man for All Seasons

Harold Brighouse Hobson's Choice

Charlotte Brontë Jane Eyre Villette

Emily Brontë Wuthering Heights

Bruce Chatwin On the Black Hill

Geoffrey Chaucer (parallel texts editions) The Nun's Priest's Tale
The Pardoner's Tale Prologue to the Canterbury Tales
The Wife of Bath's Tale

Gerald Cole Gregory's Girl

Daniel Defoe A Journal of the Plague Year

Shelagh Delaney A Taste of Honey

Charles Dickens David Copperfield Oliver Twist

George Eliot Silas Marner

T. S. Eliot Murder in the Cathedral

F. Scott Fitzgerald The Great Gatsby & Tender is the Night

E. M. Forster A Passage to India

John Fowles The French Lieutenant's Woman

William Golding Lord of the Flies

Graham Greene Brighton Rock

Willis Hall The Long and the Short and the Tall

Thomas Hardy Far from the Madding Crowd
The Mayor of Casterbridge Tess of the d'Urbervilles

Susan Hill I'm the King of the Castle

Barry Hines Kes

PAN STUDY AIDS – GCSE

▶ The complete guide to GCSE exam success

▶ Authors, are highly experienced teachers in their subjects, examiners and writers

▶ GCSE Study Aids cover all the essentials, focusing on the areas which carry the most marks and paying particular attention to common points of difficulty

▶ GCSE Study Aids supply expert guidance on how to revise and prepare for the exams

▶ GCSE Study Aids illustrate the varied types of exam questions, explaining exactly what examiners look for

▶ GCSE Study Aids give students the chance to practise their answers using sample questions supplied by the examination boards. They are regularly revised and updated

Books in the series:

GCS Biology
GCSE Chemistry
GCSE Commerce
GCSE Computer Studies
GCSE Economics
GCSE English Language
GCSE French plus tape
GCSE Geography: Book One
GCSE Geography: Book Two
GCSE German plus tape
GCSE History 1: World History since 1914
GCSE History 2: Britain and Europe since 1700
GCSE Human Biology
GCSE Mathematics
GCSE Physics
GCSE Sociology
RCN Nursing

All Pan books are available at your local bookshop or newsagent, or can be ordered direct from the publisher. Indicate the number of copies required and fill in the form below.

Send to: **CS Department, Pan Books Ltd., P.O. Box 40, Basingstoke, Hants.   RG21 2YT.**

or phone: 0256 469551 (Ansaphone), quoting title, author and Credit Card number.

Please enclose a remittance* to the value of the cover price plus: 60p for the first book plus 30p per copy for each additional book ordered to a maximum charge of £2.40 to cover postage and packing.

*Payment may be made in sterling by UK personal cheque, postal order, sterling draft or international money order, made payable to Pan Books Ltd.

Alternatively by Barclaycard/Access:

Card No. | | | | | | | | | | | | | | | | |

Signature:

Applicable only in the UK and Republic of Ireland.

While every effort is made to keep prices low, it is sometimes necessary to increase prices at short notice. Pan Books reserve the right to show on covers and charge new retail prices which may differ from those advertised in the text or elsewhere.

NAME AND ADDRESS IN BLOCK LETTERS PLEASE:

....

Name————————————————————————————

Address————————————————————————————

3/87